Love Gone Wrong

# love gone
# WRONG

## Living Happily Ever After as Survivors of Abuse

# LAUREL BAHR

with Lynn Johnson, Jillian Adams,
Mary A. Dietzen Ph. D.

NEW YORK

LONDON • NASHVILLE • MELBOURNE • VANCOUVER

# Love Gone Wrong

## Living Happily Ever After as Survivors of Abuse

Published in New York, New York, by Morgan James Publishing. Morgan James is a trademark of Morgan James, LLC. www.MorganJamesPublishing.com

ISBN 9781642797695 paperback
ISBN 9781642797701 eBook
Library of Congress Control Number: 2019949504

**Cover Design by:**
Megan Dillon
megan@creativeninjadesigns.com

**Interior Design by:**
Chris Treccani
www.3dogcreative.net

**Illustrations by:**
Kim Gardell
Gardell Design

Morgan James is a proud partner of Habitat for Humanity Peninsula and Greater Williamsburg. Partners in building since 2006.

Get involved today! Visit
MorganJamesPublishing.com/giving-back

*For my family: Mike, Kelsey, Fred, Kenney and Andrea.*
*Your love and support gave me the confidence*
*to pursue my dream of helping others.*

# TABLE OF CONTENTS:

# LETTER TO THE READER

Dear Reader,

If you have picked up this book, it's likely that you or someone you love has been sexually abused. When I was going through my recovery process, I too looked for a book to help me. I found several, and a few of them became lifelines for me. In fact, throughout the book, you'll find quotes from those I found most helpful.

However, even though these books were very informative, I never found what I was really looking for. What was that? I wanted to find a story that would give me hope, because to be honest, at the time, I had none. I couldn't see how it was possible to survive the nightmare that had become my life. Had others survived? Were there women who had healed from abuse like mine, and if so, how did they do it?

This book is the one I wish I had found and is birthed out of a desire to help others. It's my gift to you. In it, I share what happened to me, how I got better, and how I dealt with the people involved. Additionally, intertwined with my story, are two others who witnessed my recovery and were inspired to follow in my footsteps. Many of the identities of those involved have been changed in order to protect the victims and their families.

Because our stories contain vivid descriptions of emotional, physical and sexual abuse, I anticipate some readers will experience strong emotions or feel overwhelmed. Any recollections of grief or trauma that surface are an opportunity for healing. Take a step. Tell someone, or access one of the resources mentioned in the Appendix in the back of this book. You cannot heal from something you deny, suppress, or ignore.

Because the three of us are followers of Jesus, God is very much a part of our stories. However, please don't be put off by that if you don't share our beliefs. Despite any differences we may have, you can still benefit from our experiences and the things we learned.

Laurel Bahr

# INTRODUCTION

## Shocking Revelation

On November 13, 2008 I sat next to my friend Lynn on a couch in a counselor's office. We were there because I was experiencing a myriad of emotional problems like deepening depression, problems with sexual intimacy, and the final straw—a panic attack at work.

At my first appointment with the counselor, I took what felt like a huge risk. I shared a suspicion that I had been sexually molested as a child. For as long as I can remember, I believed, "something really bad happened to me." This belief was rooted in symptoms that plagued me my whole life. It's hard to speak out, even hard to write about it. Repeatedly, I would experience phantom pressure and discomfort in my mouth. These sensations would wake me in the night, and with them came anxiety. Sometimes I felt like I couldn't breathe.

---

Body Memory: "When the body remembers the traumatic incident at a different time from when the mind remembers the incident..." [1]

---

Since I couldn't remember what happened to me, I assumed I must have been a baby or toddler. I also had recurring childhood nightmares. In light of all this, I posed a question to the counselor: "Could something from my childhood be causing my current problems? I suspect that I may have been sexually abused." The answer was, "Yes."

So, here I was, on a return visit, to explore what may have happened. The counselor came and sat down across from Lynn and me. He explained that we were going to spend some time in reflection to explore that possibility.

I closed my eyes, and immediately recalled an image of myself standing on the floorboard of a truck facing what appeared to be a man's lap. I could see his genitals. I was young, maybe two. My hair was pulled back in two short curly pigtails on top of my head. The next thing I saw was my dad's face, only he appeared to be very young, like in the photos I had seen of my parents wedding day. He was laughing and smiling. As I told the counselor what was coming to mind, an image of a lollipop appeared. I knew immediately what that represented and was absolutely horrified. Waves of shame and disgust welled up inside of me. I lost all control of my emotions and began saying over and over, "What kind of girl does that?"

Unthinkable. Just completely unthinkable. I honestly never considered my dad capable of sexual abuse. He was emotionally volatile and prone to fits of rage, but not this!

I finally stopped crying long enough for my counselor to speak. "Those feelings have been there your whole life. There, but buried, along with the knowledge of what happened."

The appointment ended and as Lynn and I walked to the parking lot, I found myself unable to speak and completely undone. Once home, I crawled into my bed and wondered how I could go on with the knowledge I had had sex with my own father? Mike, my husband, got home and crawled into bed with me. Holding me tight, he reassured me we would get through this together. I wasn't so sure, and later that night I repeatedly pleaded with God to let me die.

## No Fairy Tale Ending

The next morning, my husband Mike and I sat at the kitchen counter together, the shock of the previous day's revelation was now turning into self-doubt. I began to question myself: "Was the scene in the truck a memory or something I made up?" Mike listened, but was quick to chime in, "You didn't make it up." "How do you know?" I asked. "Because I know your dad. He's a jerk." I couldn't argue with him on that point. "But that doesn't mean he sexually molested me. How could I just forget something like that?"

Although I would question myself many times in the days and months to come, I was fortunate that my husband believed me. He had been in law enforcement since he was twenty-one years old. Repressing traumatic events was something very familiar to him. Mike assured me, "I have seen it. I've taken reports from people covered in blood, who were no doubt present in a tragic accident, and yet had no memory whatsoever of being there." I listened and wasn't sure how to feel. Do I feel relieved I'm not crazy? Or distraught because it's true?

---

Repressed Memory: "Some of your childhood traumas may be remembered with incredible clarity, while others are so frightening or incomprehensible that your conscious mind buries the memory in your unconscious." [2]

---

As I dissolved once again into tears, Mike got angry. He pulled the revolver out of the waistband of his pants and set it on the counter in front of us. I stared at him. "I know you want to," I said, "But you can't kill him." Mike came back with a solid and quick, "Nothing would make me happier." I suppose deep down we both knew he wouldn't act on his feelings, but I was concerned. I made a call to our senior pastor and that afternoon we shared my new reality along with the many questions and concerns we were facing about the future. I then said something that would later become my mantra, "Well there's no fairytale ending to this story!"

## Finding Hope

In the next two years, the pieces of my past came together like a puzzle. Once fitted together, the picture told a story of severe abuse. Oddly enough, something God used in the course of my recovery was a fairytale with a happy ending: *Cinderella*. I have come to realize that I had been wrong. My story, like Cinderella's, does have a fairytale ending.

It's quite ironic really. Recently I unpacked some toys I had in storage. Most were well-used toys I had purchased for my own two kids. But there was one that had been around since my own childhood: a Cinderella doll. I got her as a gift from my parents one Christmas morning, and to be honest, was immediately disappointed. For one, I was no longer interested in dolls. Hadn't my mom noticed? And two, it was Cinderella before her "transformation." My sad-looking doll was wearing a raggedy green dress complete with a yellow patch sewn onto the skirt and an orange apron. Her blond hair was partially covered and pulled back by a matching green scarf, and in her hand was a broom! What was fun about that?

That doll, rarely taken off the shelf, remains in pretty good shape even though she is now over forty-five years old! Why my mom saved her instead of my vintage Barbie dolls, I'll never know.

I'm a grandmother now. Two of my granddaughters happen to be black. When I started stocking the house with toys for them, it made sense to me that they had black baby dolls to play with. My recent experience got me thinking…. was there something about the raggedy Cinderella that reminded my mom of me?

Cinderella, her fairytale familiar to most of us, is beloved by many. The beautiful, kind girl trapped in unfair circumstances is rescued by the prince who falls madly in love with her. The story ends with the Prince whisking her away to his palace, where the two are wed and live happily ever after as King and Queen. On the surface, it appears that Cinderella's good fortune happens *to* her: the fairy godmother gives her a dramatic makeover, the prince falls in love with her, and her friends unlock the door so she can try on the glass shoe that identifies her as the one the prince loves.

But if you look more closely, there's more to Cinderella's fairytale ending than just good fortune. Her transformation was a result of what happened *inside* her over the course of her story. Cinderella made choices. She took deliberate steps that led her on a journey from being a victim of an abusive relationship to a bride who was loved, wanted, and chosen. Her story is my story, and it could be your story too.

# 1

# The Servant

Ella began life adored and cherished by a loving father. When they were separated by his untimely death, she had **no choice** but to live with her cruel stepmother.

Ella grew up in a **harsh** environment of **selfishness** and **abuse. Favoring** her own daughters, the stepmother slowly **groomed** Ella to be the family **servant.** She cooked, cleaned and did the laundry. Eventually, they began calling her, "Cinder-ella" because she was often covered in soot from cleaning the fireplace.

However, Cinderella never complained. Instead, she survived by working hard, being kind, and holding on to her **"sweet dream."**

## 1.1 A Fiery Beginning

I was the second child born to my parents, Beverly and Larry Smith. My older sister, Debbie, had arrived two-and-a-half years before me and was born with Down's Syndrome. In the 1960s, there were no ultrasounds or blood tests during pregnancies to prepare couples for a special-needs baby. Debbie was two days old before my parents discovered anything was wrong. The doctors encouraged them to consider placing her in an institution, but my mom was adamant, Debbie would be raised at home.

This wasn't easy. Debbie's development was delayed, and both my parents worked. My mom was a schoolteacher and my dad was working towards owning his own farm. Understandably, when my mom became pregnant with me, she was very concerned about my wellbeing. However, I arrived in good health, weighing a hearty ten pounds!

After my birth, my mom's parents took Debbie to their home so mom had time to recover. Before they left, my grandmother expressed concern about the oil furnace in the home my parents were renting. It seemed to her it could not be trusted. And sure enough, two weeks later, that oil furnace, located in the nursery, blew up in the middle of the night. Our dog, sleeping next to my crib, started barking when the fire broke out. By the time my dad got to my crib, all my hair, and even my eyebrows had been singed off! It was a close call. The entire home burned to the ground in less than thirty minutes.

The fire was devastating for my folks. The furniture was new and had been bought on credit; it would be some time before it was paid off. They also lost things that can't be replaced, like wedding photos. However, my mom's reflections about the fire in the years to come were not about what they lost, but rather how her mom had been "right." She seemed to resent that. It was not the first time my grandma's warnings went unheeded, and it wouldn't be the last.

My grandma and grandfather had not wanted her to marry my dad. They warned her during the courtship that they could "see" some things in Larry that concerned them. My grandma later told me my mom spent over three days in bed after they voiced their disapproval about the engagement. In the years to come, there were times when my mom wanted to leave my dad. But stronger still was her refusal to let her mother be "right" again.

## 1.2 Favoritism and Fear

After the fire, my parents bought a chicken farm and we moved across the state to a small town called Medical Lake. We lived on the farm in an old house surrounded by a number of large, rock-walled barns spread out along a half-mile country road.

My mom got a teaching job at the junior high school, and my dad set out to make the farm a success. When I was four-and-a-half years old, my mom quit her job. Soon thereafter my parents adopted my brother Brett. Both my parents really wanted a boy, and my mom found pregnancy emotionally difficult. As the years went by, Brett enjoyed the favor of both my parents and I was treated differently as a result.

This wreaked havoc on my self-esteem. Brett was cuddly and charming from the very beginning. Conversely, my dad often said I "lived in a glass house" and was "cold." My mom, worded it differently: "You aren't very physically affectionate." In addition, throughout my childhood, my parents seemed disappointed in my appearance. Both my parents were trim and attractive, and I felt pressure to live up to their expectations.

It was not long after Brett came to live with us that Debbie and I had a life-changing experience. One Sunday, my parents unexpectedly drove into town and dropped us off at a church. Debbie and I attended the same Sunday School class. Our teacher, Mrs. Galbreath was a sweet older woman who told us about our Father in Heaven and His son Jesus. We responded by kneeling in prayer, asking Jesus to be our Savior. I think Debbie and I both felt we needed saving. Not just from our sin, but from our dad. He was very emotionally volatile and was prone to fits of rage. Our saving grace was that he was a workaholic and gone a lot. When he was home, we were terrified of him and tried to stay out of his way.

"A telling sign that something's just not right is when a child fails to seek comfort from a parent or other caregiver who is an abuser." [3]

At times, my avoidance of my dad upset him. One night my parents had a party. There was music, alcohol, and the living room was full of their friends. My dad reached down to pick me up and put me on his lap, but I would have none of it. I squirmed long and hard enough that he eventually put me down, but he was very upset. I imagine he found it embarrassing. As I made my escape from the room, one of his friends stopped me and said I had "hurt my dad's feelings." He tried to get me to go back, but I was too afraid.

In elementary school, my fear and anxiety toward my dad escalated. I was often the brunt of his anger despite my efforts to "be good." One of those occasions happened the summer between second and third grade. My parents scraped together enough money to send me to a Girl Scout camp. Although I had been looking forward to it, once there, I found myself feeling very out of place. I didn't know anyone; everyone else had arrived with ready-made friends. I also wet the bed. Each morning I was faced with the dilemma of what to do with my wet bedding and clothes. It was humiliating. I spent a lot of time in the bathroom crying and refused to do some of the activities as a result. Camp staff sent a letter home to my folks explaining my behavior.

"One of the physical warning signs of sexual abuse is soiling or wetting clothes, or bedwetting." [4]

My mom picked me up after my week-long trial. Once home, I was met with one angry and disappointed dad. Hurling one insult after the other, he scolded me for wasting their money and not participating. My mom remained silent as the word-battering continued. My crime was homesickness and the punishment was anger and rage, followed by days of the "silent treatment." That was the pattern. Never an apology, never any regret for what was said. I was just treated like I didn't matter and didn't exist... until the next time I messed up.

Not surprisingly, most of the time I believed my dad didn't like me. But with my mom, that was a different story. My mom was very sweet, loving, and had a soft and stable disposition. I don't believe she ever raised her voice at me when I was growing up. There was one time, just once, that she swore and that was in a store when my brother was acting up. It was so unusual, I never forgot it!

When I was ten and Debbie was twelve, my parents decided to let her move into a nearby institution called Lakeland Village. It was only a couple miles away from our home, and Mom, Brett, and I went there often to see her.

These visits to see Debbie were unforgettable. One step inside her dorm-like home, and we were immediately surrounded by every other girl who lived there. They flocked around us, hugging and even kissing, until the caretakers peeled them away! They had so much love to give! Debbie seemed to thrive there. Unlike in the neighborhood where I was her only playmate, at Lakeland she had many "friends." Lakeland also offered an in-ground pool, merry-go-round, and campus store. Although I missed her, the change did free me up to spend time with my friends without feeling like I was leaving her out.

## 1.3 History Repeated

I have often marveled how the things my dad didn't like about his own childhood were repeated in mine. He too suffered from mistreatment and favoritism.

My dad was from the Spokane area. He was the only child and very young when his parents divorced. His mom remarried multiple times. During her third marriage, she adopted a girl who eventually became her clear favorite. Dianna, like my brother Brett, received more attention, support, and grace than her older sibling, my dad.

The favoritism was very painful for him and so was his mother's anger. She was sharp-tongued, critical, and often launched into verbal attacks for very minor offenses. Her hostile demeanor resulted in four failed marriages. Her fifth husband, Lloyd, liked my dad a lot. He was a sweet man when sober, but violent when drunk.

My dad's biological father was another story. Although he also knew how to "tie one on," grandpa was funny, and always the life of the party! After the divorce he remarried and fathered three more children.

My dad got along well with his father, and growing up we visited their home on a regular basis. One night, while the adults played cards around the kitchen table, Debbie and I retreated to a back bedroom to watch TV. Later that night, my uncle Steve (my dad's step brother), came into the room. The room was dark, and Debbie and I were on the bed. Steve began to describe a sexual act. He told me it was "fun" and suggested we try it. But, when he pulled down his pants and exposed himself, I slipped off the bed, and escaped into the kitchen. I stood there the remainder of the night.

---

"Approximately 30% of children who are sexually abused are abused by family members. The younger the victim, the more likely it is that the abuser is a family member." [5]

---

## 1.4 A Sweet Dream

My dad made a career change the middle of my fifth-grade year. They sold the farm, and we moved across the state to a suburb of North Seattle where he managed his first restaurant. As part of a large franchise, it was located on one of the busiest streets in the area. My dad worked long hours often leaving before we got up and coming home late at night. His absence was good for me. But the move was difficult because I missed my sister. Debbie stayed at Lakeland Village, and I saw her infrequently as a result.

Our new home was two houses down from a Christian family who had a girl my age. She and I became close friends and spent a lot of time at her house. I began to notice that there was a peace and gentleness there, something that was missing in my family. When her parents started to invite me to go to church with them, I found it equally appealing and joined them as often as I could. I felt welcomed and loved there.

My friend's family and church had a huge impact on me. For the first time, I had a picture of what life could be like and it gave me hope. I started to dream of the day I could have my own family, a family who loved God and loved each other.

Living in Seattle also allowed me to spend more time with my mom's parents. My grandparents, like my neighbors and the church, were warm, loving and supportive. My grandpa, a teacher and coach, was stable and steady like my mom. He enjoyed kids and sometimes opened the school gym for my cousins and me so we could play.

My grandma... well words can't express how much I adored her! She was the truth-teller, the spicy one who loved to give gifts as freely as her own opinions. I often talked privately to her about my dad and leaned on her for encouragement and advice. She saw how my dad treated my mom. Grandma disapproved, but rarely voiced anything to my folks. She knew the kind of control my dad had and was afraid of losing my mom.

## 1.5 Lonely and Depressed

We were in Seattle for a total of two years when my parents announced we were moving to Louisiana; my dad had been promoted. This was a pattern. I would be the "new girl" seven times before completing the ninth grade. Never in one place long enough to make friends, I struggled with loneliness and depression.

---

"Abusers isolate their victims geographically and socially. Geographic isolation includes moving the victim from her friends, family and support system." [6]

---

This was definitely true in Louisiana. Everything was different there and I had a very hard time adjusting. Up north, I had black friends, and didn't think a thing about our difference in skin color. But in Louisiana, I discovered a very different dynamic. For example, at lunch, the white kids sat on one side of the room and the black kids on the other. Sometimes fights broke out, and one time someone was stabbed. It was a real eye-opener.

Another adjustment I had to make was how I talked. Up north, we would say, "you guys," even when talking to a group that included girls. The first time I said, "you guys," in my new school, a rather large girl set me straight saying, "Girl, I ain't no guy! Who you calling a guy! Don't you ever call me no guy!" That same girl would later find me in the hallway after class one day and slug me in the stomach for saying the wrong thing in class.

It was a tough move. I missed my friends, church, grandparents and Debbie. I really missed her. When she came to visit during Christmas vacation, I was so excited and noticed she had changed.

While separated, Debbie had moved from Lakeland to a group home in central Washington. The couple that ran the home were Christians and Debbie was thriving there. Her speech, emotional responses, and spiritual maturity were very apparent. I smiled as she told me about her new family, her church and her love for Jesus. Somehow God had given both of us a similar experience. I knew exactly how she felt and was so happy for her. Her visit was a bright spot at a very dark time.

We were in Louisiana for seven months, and then moved to Murfreesboro, Tennessee. The neighborhood and school were an improvement, but I wasn't there long enough to put down roots or make friends. Nine months after we arrived, we moved back to Seattle. This time however, I didn't mind. I was eager to get back to the Northwest so I could be closer to Debbie. She was born with a congenital heart defect and her health was declining. I learned she was not expected to live past the age of eighteen! At the time, I was fourteen, and she was sixteen... time was ticking!

# 2

# The Victim

One day an invitation arrived from the king. He was hosting a royal ball for the prince. Immediately, Cinderella and her stepsisters began to prepare for the event, each hopeful they would capture the attention of the prince.

The stepmother provided her daughters with extravagant new gowns, shoes, and jewelry. However, Cinderella had to make do with her mother's dress, a hand-me-down. She was starting to make the necessary alterations, when the stepmother **sabotaged** her ability to get ready by adding numerous chores to her already heavy workload.

Cinderella didn't object, but worked hard all day leaving her little time to get ready. Surprisingly, thanks to the help of her friends, she emerged from her room, in time to go.

When her step mother and step sisters saw how excited and happy Cinderella was, their anger flared and they tore her dress to shreds. This act of violence made them feel **empowered** and **superior.** Cinderella, on the other hand, felt **ashamed and humiliated**. Clearly, she was not just a servant to her family's needs, she was also a **victim** who felt **powerless** to change her situation.

When her family left for the ball, Cinderella ran into the garden and wept. Her raggedy dress mirrored how she felt about herself: **used, discarded,** and **ugly**. It seemed as if all hope was lost, and her dream of being loved would never come true.

## 2.1 Walking on Eggshells

I started my ninth-grade year in Seattle but finished it in Medical Lake. The corporation my dad worked for spiraled into bankruptcy and his vision of climbing the proverbial ladder of success ended. My parents moved back to the town we had left only four years earlier, empty-handed and disillusioned. It was a stressful time and my dad's anger escalated.

Living with my dad was like "walking on eggshells." For that reason, the first thing I would do when I saw him was "take his temperature." I'm sure my mom and brother did the same. We watched his facial expressions, noted his tone of voice, and his overall demeanor. If he was touchy and irritable, we were quiet and extra cautious. It was best not to say or do anything that would trigger a blow-up. Usually, what set him off was something very minor, and really not the main thing bothering him. The magnitude of his reaction would vary, it could be sublte and sarcastic or loud and profane.

---

"Victims will slowly lose their sense of self because they are being continually conditioned to only focus outside of themselves. They have learned to be hypervigilant to the feelings and reactions of others and have stopped focusing on their own internal feelings." [7]

---

My mom and I used to marvel at how my dad could get so angry, be so hateful, and then two seconds later act like nothing had happened. In fact, he seemed rather "happy" after he let off steam. Meanwhile, we were left behind in a puddle on the floor. I usually got the silent treatment for a day or two following an outburst from my dad. When he was ready, he would speak to me again, but there was never any remorse or apology.

## 2.2 My Mom's Friend

I am not sure why, but for some reason, I never noticed how poorly my dad treated my mom until he lost his job. By then I was fifteen and unlike the stereotypical teenager, I really liked my mom. It was hard to see her mistreated. The longer he was out of work the more things escalated, and it felt like the frequent blow-ups were getting out of control. I remember worrying where it was all headed.

Fortunately, some relief came when my dad took on a new business venture. He liked change, and was energized by a new vision. He bought a restaurant in a small town nearby. The building had fallen into disrepair, but after a major remodel and rebranding it reopened as "Willow Springs Station." It served all three meals, and alcohol in the adjacent lounge. My dad, true to form, worked hard seven days a week through the dinner hour. The reward was almost immediate; the restaurant was a success.

Meanwhile, my mom renewed her teaching certificate and was hired at the elementary school to teach third grade. She was a very conscientious employee and mom. Every night she brought papers home to grade, and made a nice family dinner for my brother and me. Once or twice a week she visited my dad at the restaurant and had dinner with him.

It wasn't long before the distance created by my dad's job took a toll on their marriage. By this time, my friendship with my mom had deepened and I was now her confidant. It was a strange role. She called me "strong" and asked me, a high schooler, for advice. In turn, I felt a responsibility to be there for her. Outside of her mom and two sisters, she really had no close friends of her own. Not that she didn't try. She did. But my dad always made her "pay" for it.

For example, one time she got invited to take golf lessons with a group of coworkers. I don't think she had much interest in the sport, but rather viewed it as a fun way to build relationships. My dad initially supported the idea, but when it was obvious she was enjoying herself without him, things changed. There were insults, complaints, and eventually she stopped going.

But, my mom had me. Every Saturday morning, there we were at the kitchen counter, rehashing the previous week's trials and sorrows. Nothing seemed to be off-limits. She talked about his moodiness, short temper, inappropriate outbursts, and other hurts. I even heard about how she felt about my dad's sexual requests... awkward! This wasn't the only time I felt she lost sight of the fact I was her daughter. More than once, she told me, "We should have never had kids." This hurt me deeply.

---

"In role reversal, the child becomes the adult, and the parent becomes the child. Victims are expected to take care of their parents, along with the other children in the family."[8]

---

When I told my grandma about my mom's regrets and how it made me feel, she responded, "You know what she meant by that," and I suppose I did. I think my mom regretted the stormy environment we kids were raised in, but not enough to do something about it.

So, for many years, my mom talked, and I listened. And I suppose that is what made me feel like we were close. It wasn't until I was much older, that I realized instead of feeling taken care of by my mom, I had grown up feeling she needed me to take care of her.

## 2.3 Unfaithful

My dad started to come home later and later and was spending a lot of time with Patsy. Patsy worked the evening shift in the restaurant lounge. She was pretty, in a cheap sort of way. She had bleached blond hair, was very tall and skinny, wore a year-round fake tan, lots of make-up, and skin tight everything with spike heels. Need I say more?

One night, my mom confronted my dad about Patsy. The two of them were in the kitchen while I was around the corner, out of sight, listening in. My mom complained, "You're never home, and when you are, you're unhappy." "Bev," he said, "You knew I wasn't a family man when you married me." She continued, "Well, you can't tell me that there isn't anything going on with her." My dad responded, "Well, I admit that some feelings have developed, but we have not acted on them."

That was enough for me. I retreated to my bedroom, furious. How could he? I never told my mom I overheard that conversation, but it didn't matter, she told me. I encouraged her, like any "friend" would, that my brother and I would support any decision she made, including leaving my dad.

---

"Most offenders are sexually compulsive. They have sex frequently and with a variety of people." [9]

---

Later that week, my mom came home, opened a bottle of wine, and with a very determined tone of voice announced she was meeting my dad at a restaurant that evening to discuss separating. I tried not to let my enthusiasm show, though I'm not sure I pulled that off. She left, they met, and the next day a large bouquet of roses showed up on the kitchen table. It was obvious how that meeting went.

I never heard my mom talk about leaving him again. What she did continue to do however, is share her problems and disappointments with me.

## 2.4 Sabotaged

Medical Lake High School was small, which made getting involved and making friends easy for most kids. However, all the moves and years without close friends had eroded any confidence I had in my "likability." Fortunately, God put people like Mickey in my path.

Mickey worked in the high school front office. On my first day of school, she escorted me to class and several days later followed up with an invitation to church. I attended the next Sunday and for the remainder of my high school and college years. This older congregation became like family; I loved them and felt loved back.

My loyalty to God and church did not bode well with my dad. He seemed quite irritated that I was a Christian and occasionally made his disapproval known through insults and little digs. One day he came home very angry at a business associate who attended my church. I was guilty by association. He raged at me for things this man had done and gave me the silent treatment for days.

---

"Profile of an Abuser: Anger and judgment are combustible, driving forces within him but are seldom directed appropriately. Rather, he tends to project his negative emotions onto whatever objects and people happen to be nearby when feelings overwhelm him." [10]

---

I suppose my dad's opposition to my faith made me more determined than ever to follow God. I continued to faithfully attend the mid-week youth group and Sunday morning services. That is, until my dad tried to sabotage my efforts and I was forced to make a choice.

I had been waitressing at my dad's resaurant since it opened. Out of the blue, he started to schedule me to work on Sunday mornings. I was furious. He knew I loved going to church. I tried to negotiate, and asked him nicely if he could change the schedule. I even offered to work Sunday afternoons instead. No surprise, my request resulted in an angry outburst. "Who the hell are you to tell me what to do?" Ultimately, I was told if I didnt like the schedule I could quit.

I was distraught, and decided to confide in my pastor. Taking his advice to heart, I drove to the restaurant and asked my dad if he had time to talk. We sat across from each other in a booth and I said, "Dad, I love God and I really enjoy going to church. It's important to me. But God commands us to respect and obey our parents. So, if you want me to work on Sundays I will."

My dad shocked me with his response. He cried! After wiping his tears, he changed the subject and began to complain about his relationship with my mom. He said he "wasn't happy." I couldn't believe it. Now both of my parents were confiding in me! I was sixteen, what was I supposed to do? I tried to point him to God, and urged him to consider marriage counseling. That never happened. Counseling was in his words, "for the weak."

I honestly think my dad could have benefited from some sort of medication. He was as up and down as a yo-yo. My mom and I used to wish we could sneak something to him on the sly. How many times did we have that conversation? He refused to look in the mirror and instead pointed the finger at everyone else for his unhappiness.

Following my sit-down meeting with my dad, I continued to work Sundays mornings until a short time later, when he changed my schedule. Fighting for what I believed in made me appreciate it even more.

## 2.5 Valued and Devalued

My involvement in church was not the only way I coped with my unhappy home life. In high school, for the first time in my life, I developed a large group of friends. Karen, a friend I made shortly after moving back, was largely responsible for this. She was very outgoing and encouraged me to try new things. Together we joined tennis and volleyball. Soon, we were hanging out with our teammates, included in sleep-overs, and had an active social calendar.

My mom was very supportive of my extracurricular activities. She attended games, matches, and award ceremonies, but she did so alone. My dad did come to one volleyball game. He sat on the bleachers with a transistor radio in his hand and listened to a football game the entire time. I heard his message loud and clear: "I'm here, but I don't want to be."

"The scapegoated child in the family is the rejected one or the child who was picked out to be abused. They feel different and abandoned." [11]

Conversely, my brother had a different experience with my dad. Dad was quite a fan of Brett. He attended games and events even when they were out of town. Of course this was hard for me to understand and my resentment grew. I began to keep a list of the ways my dad hurt me and longed for the day I could leave home.

I had a plan; I was going to become a nurse. This decision came on the heels of my sister's open-heart surgery. The whole family was at her bedside the day of her surgery. Although I was relieved there was something they could do to extend her life, watching the staff wheel her into surgery was terrifying. I couldn't help but wonder if it was going to be the last time I saw her.

Thankfully, everything went well and after she got out of recovery, we were allowed to visit her in the Cardiac Care Unit. When we entered the room, Debbie was on a ventilator, and incoherent. I looked around the room, and couldn't believe how many tubes, lines, and machines there were. I was completely fascinated. I began asking the nurse questions, completely unaware that my parents had become faint and left the room. Later, I found them sitting on chairs in the hallway drinking orange juice. Apparently, they didn't find the experience as thrilling as I did!

I owe my sister so much. Nobody in my life influenced me more than she did. This would not be the last time that her pain changed the direction of my life.

## 2.6 Exerting Control

When I was a junior in high school, I began dating Mike. I had gone out with other guys here and there, but Mike was my first love. Our relationship started the E-Harmony way, before E-Harmony existed. A friend and I sat at her dining room table with our school yearbook, slowly examining each male classmate's photo. Why? I needed a date for the upcoming Winter Festival Dance. All my friends were going, and I didn't want to be left out. We started in the A's, and only got as far as the B's. "Bahr, Mike Bahr," my friend said. "Now he would treat any girl like a queen."

That was enough for me! I didn't know Mike, but after that endorsement I sure wanted to. Even better, he was taller and weighed more than I did! My friend and I spent the rest of the evening discussing a strategy designed to get Mike's attention. Although the first plan failed miserably, a mutual friend came to my rescue. He introduced the two of us, and then without skipping a beat, told Mike I was his date for the dance. I was horrified and thrilled all at the same time.

We had a great time at the dance, but when Mike drove me home things went south. Like a gentleman, he walked me to the door and we stood outside... for a very long time! Mike told me one funny story after another, which was fine, except it was a very cold December night and I had on a knee-length dress. When there was a lapse in our conversation, I saw my window of opportunity. I leaned forward and he leaned forward.... and then... I naively licked him. I could defend myself by saying that my first kiss had been a French one, so I thought it was done that way all the time. But, let's face it, I still licked him!

I went into the house confident I would never hear from him again. But much to my surprise, Mike called the next day and every day for the following three months. We were inseparable "friends"... but no kissing!

Mike and I spent a lot of time at his house. We trained for sports, played cards, backgammon, and ate junk food. His mom stocked her pantry well, it was a teenager's delight! We had as much pizza, Ding Dongs, chips, and pop as we wanted. For some reason, his parents welcomed me with open arms. To be honest, sometimes I wasn't sure who liked me more, Mike or his parents.

The longer we dated, the less I was home, and the more insecure my dad got. One night, I came in five minutes past my curfew. No joke, five minutes. I went to my bedroom, and my parents followed, my dad screaming in a full-blown rage. He accused me of having sex with Mike and boasted of my mom's virginity before they married. I was very angry and hurt. This was not how Brett was treated. He could come home late, drunk, be hung-over at the restaurant the next day for work and get a pat on the back. It was a complete double-standard.

## 2.7 A Departure

After high school, I went away to college. I had mixed feelings about it. On one hand, I couldn't wait to be away from my dad. On the other hand, I was very concerned about leaving my mom. Who would be there for her when I was gone?

My mom was working the day I moved into the dorm, and my dad was angry he had to take me. When we reached the dorm, he stopped the car, quickly off-loaded my stuff onto the curb, and took off. I couldn't help but notice how some of the parents were helping lug all their kid's belongings to their new room while still others were engaged in long embraces and tearful goodbyes.

The stark contrast reinforced the confusion and pain I felt. I graduated from high school with a 3.95 GPA, didn't drink, didn't do drugs, and worked for my own spending money. I was helpful around the house, often doing things without being asked. So, what was wrong with me? Why did he treat me like this? I could never figure it out.

I changed my name the first week after moving into the dorm. Although my legal name is Laurel, my parents had started calling me Laurie when I was a toddler. I didn't want to go by Laurie anymore. Instead, I referred to myself as Laurel. I liked Laurel, it was unique, and a departure from my past.

My new name and new address didn't exactly lead to a "new and improved life" however. Without Karen and Mike, who were both attending different colleges, I found myself withdrawing back into the familiar shell of my childhood. This only worsened when Mike broke things off during a visit, two months into my first term. I sank into a deep depression and wondered if I would ever find someone who would love me like he did.

Like other times in my life, in desperation, I pressed into God. I joined a campus Christian group and nearby church. Most of my time, however, I spent studying and going to class. I was in the pre-nursing program and found the coursework very difficult. The competition to get into nursing school was stiff, and my grades had to be exceptional.

## 2.8 A Second Chance

Near the end of my sophomore year I was accepted into the nursing program, which meant moving back to Spokane. This triggered thoughts about Mike. It had been a year and eleven months since we had broken up, but who was counting? I was! The entire time I was away at college, I thought about him. No one else I dated ever seemed to measure up. So, I contrived a trip home to return a hat he had left at a friend's house, in hopes it would lead to a reunion.

My plan was more successful than I could have dreamed. Mike's dad, who was still in my court, was home when I dropped by with the hat. Before I knew it, his dad invited me to go with them for Chinese food. One thing led to another, and Mike and I spent almost the whole weekend together. It was pretty romantic, and it turned out he never forgot me either.

To be honest, Mike didn't stand a chance. When we broke up, he took down the framed picture of the two of us positioned on the TV in the living room. However, his mom found it and put it back. They repeated this cycle a number of times before Mike finally gave up. For the entire time we had been broken up, every time he watched TV, there I was staring right back at him.

Not surprisingly, Mike's family welcomed me back home that summer with open arms. I worked at my dad's restaurant, while Mike graduated with his AA in law enforcement and looked for a job. I was happy, and so in love.

## 2.9 Don't Talk

There was one person who wasn't happy about my relationship with Mike and that was my dad. One day after work my dad unexpectedly berated me for putting my foot on the rail of a chair when taking an order at the restaurant. He then became irate over the fact I had spent eighty dollars on a watch, which I had bought with my own money for nursing school.

And then, I suspect the real issue surfaced. He started yelling something about how I liked spending time with Mike's dad and suggested maybe Mike's dad would help pay for my school. He was jealous!

All of it was utterly absurd, and I started to yell back, which of course only made him angrier. We both swore, called each other names, and it ended with my dad storming out of the house. But I didn't care, and I certainly didn't regret it.

However, that's not how my mom and brother felt. They both witnessed the argument and were very upset with me. "Why did you do that?" my mom asked. "What do you mean, why? He was being ridiculous!" I replied. "But," she said, "you knew he was wrong."

---

"Each family member is in one of three roles: offender, denier, or victim. Deniers believe the best way to survive is to ingratiate themselves with the offenders in the family and keep a low profile. They know who has the power in the family, and they work diligently to stay on the good side of the offender." [12]

---

You knew he was wrong… but be quiet? This was my mom's philosophy on how to manage my dad's irrational and angry behavior. He could literally say or do anything he wanted, and she refused to fight back. She just took what he dealt out and called it "peace." And she expected us to do the same. Too many times to count she told me not to cry, disagree, or show emotion when faced with my dad's unreasonable or violent behavior.

Although I could see my mom didn't approve of my new bravado, I was determined to stand up for myself despite the cost.

## 2.10 A Dream Come True

Mike and I dated for six months, and then got engaged at Christmas. He bought me a ring, wrapped it in a small box, then put that in a slightly bigger box, and wrapped that, and so on. Christmas Eve, with all his family watching, I opened one box after the other and was thrilled to find a beautiful gold engagement ring. It seemed fitting to celebrate with all my "supporters" gathered around!

We set the date for the wedding and started making the needed preparations. Although I was determined to enjoy the experience, things got off to a disappointing start when my parents told me they weren't going to buy me a dress. Instead, I was expected to find one to borrow. Since I didn't have the money to buy my own, I had no choice but to go along. Fortunately, Mike's older sister offered to let me borrow hers. It was not my style, but nice. The only problem was, Cheryl was 5'10" and I was 5'6". I found the tallest pumps I could and prayed I wouldn't trip and fall during the wedding.

We kept things simple overall. Mike asked my brother Brett, and three of his friends to stand up for him. Meanwhile, I picked out the bridesmaid dresses and asked Karen, two of Mike's sisters, and Debbie to be in the wedding. Debbie was so excited!

Our short, two-month engagement went by very quickly. Unfortunately, the entire time, my dad continued to maintain that "I could do better." My dad cared a lot about money and status; he had a real problem with Mike's chosen "blue collar" profession. At our wedding rehearsal dinner, he gave the traditional toast and said something to the effect of, "Here's to Mike and Laurel, we can only hope that someday Mike will grow up and get a real job." Of course, I was furious, as was Mike's family, many of whom were working in law enforcement at the time. I went home that night wishing we had just eloped.

The next day, things went fairly well with a few exceptions. The photographer arrived drunk. That was unfortunate! And the whole experience of walking down the aisle with my dad was awkward. As we stood in the back of the church, waiting for our cue. I could tell he was trying to create some sort of tender moment between the two of us. It was a nice gesture; the problem was, I just couldn't reciprocate.

Once down the aisle, I was standing next to Mike facing the cross in the very church that years before I had made a similar commitment to love Jesus. Finally, I was with a man who loved me and treated me like a "queen." We said our vows. I gave him my heart and he gave me his. My sweet dream of having a family that loved each other and loved God was starting to come true.

# 3

# Loved

Suddenly, Cinderella's fairy godmother appeared! With one wave of her wand, she gave her a magical makeover. Her raggedy dress was transformed into a stunning gown and on her feet were one-of-a-kind tiny glass slippers. With another wave of her wand, Cinderella's animal friends became her personal attendants.

With no time to waste, she climbed into her magical coach. But before departing, the fairy godmother warned Cinderella saying, "At the stroke of midnight, the spell will be broken, and everything will be as it was before."[13]

The last to arrive at the ball, Cinderella felt surprisingly confident, thanks to her magical makeover. She stepped onto the ballroom floor and greeted the prince with a low curtsey, accepting his invitation to dance. The prince was captivated by her beauty, and together, they whirled across the dance floor. Soon, it was obvious to all, that Cinderella had won the **favor** of the prince.

The effect this had on Cinderella was profound. Instead of feeling ashamed, scorned, and rejected, **she felt admired, sought after and cherished.** Like her crystal-clear slippers, her new identity as "the one the prince loves" fit her perfectly.

### 3.1 Given Grace

The honeymoon lasted one night. We got married on a Saturday, moved into our tiny one-bedroom apartment on Sunday, and on Monday were back in class. Mike was attending the Police Academy, and I was in my second semester of nursing school. To some it may have appeared rushed, but not to us. We were so excited to be married. However, little did we know that just around the corner was a potential separation.

It all started on what seemed like a pretty normal day on campus. I was in class waiting for a lecture to start, when a courier surprised me with a certified letter from the United States Army. I opened it immediately, and discovered I was being charged with a crime! Willful Evasion! A trial date was listed, and it was noted that if found guilty, I would be immediately sent to boot camp. What had I done?

I had joined the Army my freshman year of college after Mike and I broke up. I suppose it was my way of putting a flag in the sand and declaring I was fully capable of moving on alone. I didn't need Mike, and I certainly didn't need my dad or his money. I applied for and was awarded a four-year Army Nurse Corp Scholarship.

I'm sure I would have kept my four-year commitment after graduation, had Mike not objected. But he did. It made sense to me. He was launching his career and didn't want to move. Unsure of what to do, I sent a letter to the US Army Department, explaining my predicament as well as my intent to pay back all the money they had given me. Given the charges filed against me, it was obvious the Army didn't agree with my new plans!

The day of the trial, I put on my best suit, and traveled from nursing school down to my former campus's ROTC building. Once there, they led me into a conference room where eight Army officers were seated around a large table. After being sworn in, I took a seat and surveyed the faces of the men who held the fate of my future in their hands. One of the officers, turned on a cassette recorder and placed it in the middle of the table before beginning to read a very legal sounding document explaining why we were there. My heart was pounding, my palms sweaty as I anticipated their first question. Just then, without any warning, the entire group of middle-aged men erupted in uncontrollable laughter. I had no idea what was so funny!

It took a few minutes, but eventually they composed themselves. They rewound the tape and the court hearing was restarted. I braced myself a second time, when suddenly one of the officers started to giggle. This triggered a chain reaction and once again all the men were laughing hysterically.

Four rounds of giggles later, I finally got to answer a few questions, but by then, it was clear to me the hearing was a formality. The blissfully ignorant way I had tried to exit the Army Corp was received with grace, something I had not experienced much growing up. Although legally, these officers could have ordered me to report to boot camp, they didn't. For reasons, I cannot explain, the charges against me were dismissed and I was free to go.

**3.2 Shown Favor**

After Mike graduated from the Police Academy, I moved in with his mom so I could finish my senior year of Nursing School. Sadly, Mike's parents had divorced the year before we had married. Meanwhile, Mike moved to Omak and began working at the Police Department. Every weekend one of us made the two-and-a-half-hour drive to see the other. It was a busy time, but not so busy we didn't enjoy married life. When I graduated and moved to Omak, I was seven months pregnant with our first child.

Being a twenty-two-year-old mom was not what I had planned. After four years of college, I was eager to get my career off the ground. However, when Kelsey was born, we were instantly love-struck. Career? What career? One look at our precious daughter and nothing else really mattered that much.

A few months later, the manager of the labor and delivery unit at the only hospital in the area called me at home. She had heard through the grapevine about me and my interest in becoming a labor and delivery nurse. (I wasn't kidding when I said, "small town.") Right there on the phone, without an application or interview, despite my inexperience, she gave me the job.

I felt God's favor, paving the way for me to step into my dream job. I worked two-and-a-half years in Omak enjoying my roles as a wife, mom and labor & delivery nurse. But when Mike was offered a job at a police department near our hometown, we decided to move. Mike was excited about the opportunity to go back to school and get his four-year degree in Criminal Justice. And I hoped to work at a larger hospital with higher-risk patients.

The move was easy; we had very little to our name back then. Mike started his new job and full-time class schedule. I made one trip to the hospital of my dreams, applied for the only day position they had open, and got it! Was it really supposed to be this easy?

A year later, we were surprised by another pregnancy. As my delivery date approached, we discussed names, but couldn't agree. If it was a boy, Mike wanted to name him Kenney in honor of his dad. I on the other hand, had some trendier names in mind, like Cash or Grant. Mike objected to these and every other name I suggested. Usually he said something like "Here Cash, come here Cash! See, we can't name him that. It's a dog's name!" I'm pretty sure any name other than Kenney would have been a dog's name.

Delivery day came, and God blessed us with an eight-pound, one-ounce boy! When I saw Mike staring at our new baby boy in the delivery room, I caved. It was such a tender moment, and I knew it would mean a lot to him to name him Kenney. Must have been the hormones! Of course, the name grew on me.

Not so for Mike's mom, however. Still upset about her divorce, she referred to Kenney as "Little Sh*t" for years. (Although she did it in a way that oozed adoration.) Mike expected her to be mad, but one thing was for sure, my husband wasn't afraid to stand up to his family. This would become an important quality in later years when I would need his support to stand up in unimaginable ways to my own family. God knew what he was doing when he gave me Mike.

Mike graduated with a BA in Criminal Justice, was hired by the Spokane Police Department and was eventually promoted to Detective. His dreams, like mine, were also coming true. We put down roots and bought a brand-new home. What a thrill it was to pick out our floor plan, lot, and finishing touches. Not in my wildest dreams did I ever think this would be possible. Soon, our life looked like many others. We were immersed in raising our children, maintaining our home, and advancing our careers. It was a busy but fruitful time. I was livin' the dream, and life was good.

### 3.3 Special to God

As Mike and I neared our mid-thirties, we decided I would cut back my hours at work. My new schedule afforded me some much-needed margin, and for the first time in years, I slowed down long enough to realize that something was missing. When a friend invited me to join her women's Bible study, I enthusiastically agreed. Looking back, I believe God put me in that study knowing I was careening towards one of the most painful experiences of my life.

My sister's health had begun to decline. At this time, Debbie was living in a group home only forty-five minutes away from our home and we saw each other regularly. During our visits, she often compared our lives. I can still hear her say, "I want to be like you Laurie. I want a husband, and a job. I have dreams too." It was ironic. My precious sister wanted to be like me, but in so many ways I wanted to be like her. No, I didn't want her struggles but rather her heart. I felt she had a much better handle on the things that really mattered in life.

For instance, Debbie was passionate about her relationship with God. It was not uncommon for me to find her in her room, Bible open with a pen in hand. She liked to copy Scripture onto paper and underline the passages. She also prayed a lot and often.

My sister also valued relationships. I can't remember a greeting that didn't include a lingering bear-sized hug. Even people like my dad, who could be difficult to love, got one. I admired her for that. She remembered birthdays, often spending what little money she had on cards or gifts.

In her mid-thirties, Debbie started dating Chris. The two of them lived at the same group home and were an adorable couple. When they announced their engagement, both sets of parents agreed to support their decision as did their church!

The pastor met with them regularly and they completed premarital counseling. The women of her church hosted a shower. My mom got busy and made her a dress, and I contributed by creating her bouquet and veil. She had a beautiful, well-attended church wedding, a traditional honeymoon, then she and Chris resumed life at the group home as husband and wife.

When Debbie and Chris had been married about a year she was hospitalized for pneumonia. They treated her with IV antibiotics and released her a few days later. However, this became the first of multiple episodes all having similar presenting symptoms: fluid in her lungs, shortness of breath, and an infection. I began to get suspicious. It just wasn't adding up.

One night, during one of these hospital admissions, Mike and I arrived to find her crying and upset. The nurse was having trouble starting her IV and Debbie had just lost it. I asked everyone to leave and sat down on the edge of her bed. I remember we talked about God, and how He cared for her. I offered to pray and said I thought Jesus could help us. She replied, "Yes, when I am weak, He is strong," referring to a Bible verse she had memorized. Like I said she was very spiritually mature.

Uncomfortable with her care, I requested she be transferred to a different hospital. She was flown to Spokane and some of the best doctors in the region were assigned to my sister's case. Studies were done, labs drawn, and incredibly, they were still unable to determine the cause of her symptoms. Everyone agreed she was very sick, but no one could tell me why.

That week, I wept at Bible study as I explained my dilemma and concerns. One of the women in my small group asked, "Have you asked

God to point you to a doctor that will know what's wrong?" Without missing a beat out of my mouth came, "Well I think God's got bigger problems to deal with than that." I guess that must have been how I really felt. God loved the world, and I was just a speck in the midst of millions.

My small group prayed with me, and the next day one of my coworkers suggested I talk to a neonatal heart specialist about my sister's condition. She said, "Dr. Garabedian operates on babies with Downs Syndrome, he might be helpful." I pushed past my insecurities and went right then, in my scrubs to his office. He welcomed me in, and after ten minutes of describing my thirty-seven-year-old sister's condition he said, "She has right-sided heart failure." I told him, "She's had ultrasounds to rule out heart failure." Without missing a beat, he said, "They were looking at the left side, your sister has right-sided heart failure." Dr. Garabedian knew Debbie's doctor personally. He picked up the phone, called him, and confirmed his suspicions. No one had looked at the right side of her heart. I was dumbfounded.

Studies were ordered and the diagnosis was confirmed. What was also confirmed? That Jesus loved the world, but He also loved me. I was important to Him. If I prayed specifically, I was more aware how He was answering. This was a pivotal moment in my relationship with Jesus.

## 3.4 Caretaking

Dr. Garabedian agreed to be her primary doctor, and I began to make plans to move Debbie to our home. Chris, her husband had done a lovely job taking care of her, but Debbie was on oxygen, weak, and needed more help than he could give.

Mike acquired a hospital bed from a coworker, I cleared out the office on our main floor, and then went to get my sister. It was a raining hard that day, the gray skies mirroring how we all felt. Watching the goodbye between Chris and Debbie was unforgettably heart-wrenching. It was like a scene out of a very sad love story.

We got Debbie settled at our house, but less than a week later my mom showed up unannounced. She was not her soft-spoken self. Instead, in a very determined tone, she voiced, "Your dad and I have decided to take Debbie home with us."

Bombshell dropped. She left, and I was all kinds of things like angry, confused, and hopeless. I did not think my parents were capable of caring for Debbie. They had avoided almost all her hospitalizations. I tried my best not to judge them for it. If they didn't want to see her health declining, who could blame them? Yet all I could think was, "Now you want to be involved? After I have done all this work to get her settled in my home?" Of course, I didn't say what I was thinking. It never occurred to me to tell my mom "No," or try to change her mind. I did what I had always done, I complied and acted nice.

I told Debbie the news, she cried, begging me to let her stay. I did my best to be optimistic about the change in plans and reminded her how much mom and dad loved her. Then I went to my own bedroom and cried like I have never cried before.

Shortly afterwards, we loaded up the hospital bed, medication and equipment, and moved her to my parents' house. It didn't take long before I received numerous calls from my mom who was overwhelmed with Debbie's care. I did what I was used to doing, I played the role of caretaker, took a leave of absence from work, left my kids and husband, and went to stay with Debbie... at my parents' house.

## 3.5 Homegoing

To say being at my folks was hard is an understatement. The responsibility of caring for Debbie, coupled with being the target of my dad's volatile mood swings brought about a lot of anxiety. But I would do it again in a heartbeat because of the memories I made with Debbie. Debbie and I talked about heaven, what it would be like, and how she would get to see Jesus face-to-face. During the last few months of Debbie's life, God continued to meet every need I had in amazing ways. But nothing compared to what He did the day Debbie died.

June 1st. That was the day Debbie's kidneys and other systems started to shut down. Consequently, she was too weak to move any of her muscles, she couldn't even swallow. Trying to keep her comfortable, I took a straw and dribbled little drops of water into her very dry mouth from time to time. Although she didn't have the energy to talk, she was alert. When she drifted off to sleep, I remained on one side of her bed. My mom's parents sat on the other side. I was so grateful they had come. I was not alone. My parents? Well, my mom was at the kitchen counter with my dad, who was upset and talking about work.

Then it happened. Suddenly, after being asleep for an hour or so, Debbie sat up in the bed all on her own. Her bright eyes were fixed on the ceiling, and she was beaming. I wasn't sure what was going on, and asked, "Debbie do you need something?" She didn't acknowledge me but continued to gaze upwards. Suddenly, she said, "Ok, I'm coming home. Yeah, I'm coming home. Ok, I'm coming home." As soon as the words were out of her mouth, she fell back limply into the bed.

My grandparents and I looked at each other in disbelief. It was obvious we had just witnessed something supernatural. I was dumbfounded! For months, I had reassured Debbie saying, "Jesus is going to come, take you by the hand, and the two of you will go to heaven." I believed it, I just never in a million years thought I would get to see it!

My sister's death, like her life, was a gift from God. In *losing* Debbie, one of the most important people in my life, I *found* a deeper more personal relationship with Jesus. He was not just my Savior; He had become my friend. Once again, Debbie's pain became my gain.

### 3.6 Chosen

I thought I was prepared for Debbie's death. But it turned out to be much more painful than I ever imagined. I leaned into my relationship with Jesus, and a new desire emerged. One day as I was leaving Bible study, I told God, "I want You to use me, I want my life to make a difference." It was my "Jesus-take-the-wheel" moment. I know He heard me because in less than a year-and-a-half my life was almost unrecognizable. In fact, on many mornings, the first thought I had was, "Who am I and how did I get here?"

It all began when we visited a new church. The kids both loved it immediately. We started attending regularly and Mike and I even took an adult discipleship class together. We usually don't agree on much: I say black, he says white. Why do opposites attract anyhow?

The pastors leading our class announced they were planting a church on the north side of Spokane, near our home, and asked us to pray about helping them. We did, and once again, we both agreed.

The new church launched and soon Mike and I were in over our heads. While I helped with the coffee bar, Mike recruited a team of volunteers who met him early on Sunday mornings after he got off the night shift. They pulled a trailer containing all the equipment necessary to set up our portable church in a nearby middle school. It took the team three hours to set up and tear down, and in between we held two services for about 500 people. It was a big commitment, but one we felt good about.

After several months, the senior pastor and his wife asked me to lead Women's Ministry. I was very surprised and couldn't understand why they would choose me. There were other more mature Christian women on our church-planting team. Although I did my best to try to bring them to their senses, they insisted I pray about it. As I did, I was reminded of my prayer for God to use me. Scared out of my mind, I accepted the role.

## 3.7 Letting Go

As our lives became immersed in the church, I found it increasingly difficult to maintain my hours at the hospital. I was only working part-time, but my church role required about 30 hours a week. Between both jobs, it was a lot. And then it started, this nagging thought that I was supposed to step away from my career.

I dismissed the notion for months. It was utterly ridiculous. I made great money and nursing was my passion. I was not giving it up. However, when I began to have a hard time getting shifts despite my seniority, I began to wonder if the "utterly-ridiculous" idea was in fact from God.

The struggle to put together a schedule around my ministry commitments continued. It was as if I was in a wrestling match with God.

And let's just say, I lost. One day at work, this thought kept going through my head: "I want you go to church tonight, and I'm going to tell you to leave your job. And then we'll be done having this discussion."

I cried off and on all day, then went home and cried again to Mike. My dramatic presentation did not move him, however. It rarely did. Instead, he said, "Maybe you should go upstairs and take a nap." I did, nothing changed, and later I went to church.

When it was time for the message, the pastor got up and preached about an encounter between Peter and Jesus. In this story Jesus challenged Peter to lay down his fishing career to "feed God's sheep." The pastor elaborated, "Some of you here are being asked by God to leave your jobs and go into vocational ministry. God says to you, it's time to do what I want you to do; you need to let go."

A blubbering mess, I now knew without a shadow of a doubt what God was asking me to do, and I also knew I couldn't tell Him no. But, maybe Mike could? The more I thought about it, the more certain I was that Mike would never agree to let go of my nursing income.

Wrong! I told Mike what happened, and he agreed to pray together about our future. We decided if we could sell our home by owner, pay off the car, find another house we could afford on one income, and keep the kids in the same school district, then I would quit.

I was very skeptical. That was a lot of "ifs." We started by listing the house for top dollar in the newspaper the following weekend. It sold.

The same weekend the house sold, we heard of a group of homes nearby being auctioned off at below market value. We called the realtor and he met us there. One by one, we made our way through the neighborhood. It was depressing. I thought I had prepared myself for the fact our future home would be older and smaller. But as we walked through the houses, I started to feel sick. I was leaving a six-year-old home that was our choice of lot, floor plan, and finishing touches. I had perennial gardens I had nursed from seeds, and rooms I decorated with care. It was one thing to think about losing my career, now my home too?

Driving up to one rancher on two acres of land, I had this thought: "I am giving you this house." Where did that come from? Did I want this house? The exterior looked very dated. The many flower beds were overgrown with weeds. Tears stung my eyes, and for reasons I can't explain. It somehow felt like a gift. Mike looked at me and asked what was wrong. I blurted out: "God just told me He is giving us this house." Mike's response: "Well, do you still want to see the inside?" Gotta love that guy!

Inside the home, the tears continued to flow. The kitchen cupboards were warped, the tile ugly, the woodwork dark and depressing. But I could see us there. Mike liked it too, and at the end of the silent auction, we received the news our offer was accepted.

There was just one problem… we were asked to sign a "smell clause" or odor easement. That's right. Apparently, that's why the houses were on the market. The development had sued the city because a compost site across the highway was creating a very rank smell that drifted into the neighborhood. It smelled like rotten eggs and was worse in the summer. The realtor was optimistic however, because our home came with air conditioning. "As long as you keep your windows closed, you should be fine," he said. All I could think was, "Dear God, what are we doing!"

Did I already say I was sick to my stomach? Not from the smell, mind you. We were purposefully, of our own free will, giving up our home, my career, and dreams to move to a smelly neighborhood so I could be unemployed. Were we crazy? Apparently so.

Once settled into the smelly house, I gave two weeks' notice, and prepared myself to "let go." Thirty minutes before my last shift was to end, my patient's labor unexpectedly took off. The baby was born at exactly the end of my shift, 3:30 on the dot. In my heart, I had this sense of, "It is finished," and was confident God was speaking through my circumstances. He had given me one last baby to deliver; I was done being a nurse.

## 3.8 A New Passion

I grieved both the loss of my career and my sister's death, while throwing myself into my volunteer work at the church. The women's ministry began small, but over time the studies grew and soon the need emerged for more volunteers. I began asking for help, and the women responded. Some helped teach, some led small groups, still others worked with the children. Teams emerged and so did a new passion for ministry development. I really enjoyed mobilizing and training volunteers to serve in the area of their greatest strength.

What else did I enjoy? The women! I made so many friends during this time. Two of them, Lynn and Jillian would be by my side for many years.

**Jillian:** I met Jillian at the kickoff event for Women's Ministry. I was very nervous that night. Although I had taught prenatal classes for years at the hospital, the thought of speaking to a group of women about God was very intimidating. I worked on my talk for days leading up to the event and hoped the women would find it inspiring.

Jillian came up to me afterwards, introduced herself, and said God put it on her heart to pray for the ministry and me. Her words touched my heart, and we began to meet regularly for prayer. Our relationship grew, and eventually we discovered Jillian's birthday was the same day as Debbie's and we've thought of each other as sisters ever since. Jillian, like Debbie, was very upbeat, caring, and complimentary. A single mom of two, she never complained and often boasted of God's faithful provision. She was a cheerleader who loved to focus on encouraging others.

I met **Lynn** when she began attending the Bible study with her husband's grandmother. When I discovered she lived in my neighborhood, I pursued a relationship with her. We began going for walks, met for coffee, and occasionally got our families together for dinner. Lynn was a rare find. She was articulate, wise, and able to connect with me on a deep level about subjects that mattered to me. We talked often about our faith, families, and everyday challenges.

Later that Spring, I asked Lynn to be a small group leader at the Bible Study. The women looked up to her, and she navigated delicate situations well. When I began to pray about leaving my role in Women's Ministry to start a Special Needs Ministry, Lynn seemed to be the obvious choice to replace me. Although reluctant at first, I asked her to teach one of the lessons near the end of the session. Her teaching was insightful, and the women easily embraced her as the new leader.

During the two years I volunteered, I was surprised how my talents and abilities could be used not only in nursing, but in ministry as well. Letting go of nursing had been difficult, but I didn't regret it. God was using me, and as He did, my relationship with Him continued to grow. I was dancing with the Prince, and felt chosen, loved and special.

# 4

# Overwhelmed

The sky grew dark, and the moon began to shine overhead. For Cinderella, this was a grave reminder of her parting promise to her fairy godmother, **"I'll be home before midnight."** Time was running out, and she felt a **growing sense of fear, sorrow, and dread.** She didn't want to leave the prince, but what choice did she have? Surely, once her magical gown disappeared, he would **feel differently** about her.

## 4.1 A Juggling Act

The church was two years old when I accepted a paid position on staff. At the time, my daughter Kelsey and I were in the process of launching a ministry for special needs children. My new responsibilities led me to hand the vision off to her and she was the one who led the new program for children. Kelsey shared my passion to see the church equipped to minister to families with special needs. The program grew in no time at all. Many parents of special needs children told us they had resigned themselves to staying home on Sundays because they had been turned away from so many churches. Once again, God was using my sister's life to make a difference.

Meanwhile, I stepped into my new role as a licensed staff pastor. Most of my time and effort was aimed at teaching, coaching ministry leaders, and collaborating with other staff. I continued to form and develop teams and saw numerous ministries birthed as a result.

It was an exciting but challenging season of life. It wasn't easy juggling ministry, mothering teenage kids, and being Mike's wife, all while taking ministerial classes. My free time became very limited and I unintentionally let go of some very special girlfriends as a result. However, Jillian volunteered in the prayer ministry, so I saw her all the time. Additionally, Lynn was on my staff team, and we met regularly.

Our church grew rapidly and soon we were holding four services on the weekends. God was at work, and many lives were saved, healed and restored. Little did I know then I was about to experience God's power at work in my own life in ways I never imagined.

## 4.2 Forgiveness in My Heart

I can see now that my recovery from abuse began during my early years on staff at the church. That was when God first began to talk to me about my relationship with my dad. A few years before, my nursing unit was sent to a mandatory conference about domestic violence. In the very first session, as the instructor described the cycle of abuse, I began to connect what I was learning with the events of my childhood. Flash backs of painful family memories suddenly emerged and the tears came easily. It's amazing how, under the right circumstances, all those feelings can return.

That day, for the very first time, I realized I had been raised in an emotionally and verbally abusive home. It was painfully obvious both my mom and I had been victims! I was shocked! Even though all my memories of sexual abuse were still buried, I still had a lengthy list of other hurts I could recite at a moment's notice. The list kept the pain fresh, and consequently I erected a thick wall of emotional distance between my dad and me. I even had trouble looking my dad in the eye when speaking to him. At the conference, I learned this can be a sign of shame and abuse.

For several years, I believed I was a victim of abuse, but did nothing about it. Now, while working on the church staff, God was beginning the process of healing by asking me to forgive. I couldn't seem to escape His voice. The theme of forgiveness repeatedly showed up in messages on the radio, in books I read, in song lyrics, and in phrases that stood out in my Bible reading plan. One day, in a Bible study lecture, the speaker asked, "Who is God asking you to forgive?" Immediately, my dad came to mind, and my reaction was a strong, "I can't."

When my heart responded, "I can't," that was no joke. I couldn't even fathom how to begin to let go of all he had done. It was overwhelming to even think about it. Not knowing what else to do, I prayed and told God how I felt. I said I was willing, but He would have to do it for me. Amazingly, over time, God did just that, but it all started with my willingness to obey.

In the beginning, obedience looked like simply praying for the man. Not that I wanted to pray for him, mind you. However, as I prayed for things like his salvation and relationship with my mom, I noticed something. My feelings changed. I started to have pangs of compassion and a desire for our relationship to improve followed. It was a miracle!

These changes in my heart happened over the course of months, not days. Forgiveness was a process, and a long one. Eventually, God asked me to let go of the list. I stopped rehearsing what my dad had done to me, stopped holding it against him, and pictured myself releasing it.

## 4.3 Forgiveness Spoken

At about this time, my parents got some shocking news. My dad had a terminal illness: Myelodysplastic Anemia. Although there was no cure, through medical management we learned it was possible to prolong his life by as many as ten years.

I felt an urgency I couldn't explain, and sensed God was asking me to talk to my dad about our relationship. Since Mike and I planned to see him on his birthday, I decided to bite the bullet and talk to him then.

The evening we got ready to go to my parents' house I was optimistic. I envisioned a difficult conversation that ended well, triggering the start of a new beginning. Numerous times on the drive out to their home, a Bible verse kept coming to mind: "You intended to harm me, but God intended it all for good, He brought me to this position so I could save the lives of many people."[14] I knew Joseph said this to his estranged brothers at a dinner that ended with their reconciliation. I took the reminder as encouragement from God and believed the evening ahead was going to end well. How very wrong I was.

I waited until after dinner, and taking my dad aside, asked him if we could go into the other room to talk. We sat down at a table, and I said something to the effect of: "Dad, I have been praying a lot about our relationship. Over the years it's been very painful for me, but I have forgiven you. I just want you to know that I love you."

My dad reacted strongly to the notion he needed forgiveness and didn't hear anything else I had to say. He started to shake, stood up, pointed his finger at me, and yelled, "I don't need your forgiveness! It was all your fault! You've been cold since the day you were born! We've all talked about it."

Caught off guard, I remained sitting, and eventually said, "Dad just forget about the forgiveness part, I just wanted to tell you I love you." But it was too late. He carried on in a manner I hadn't witnessed since I was in college.

I gave up on the idea of making any progress that night and made my way to the front door. As I did, I turned, looked at him and said, "So you are going to do to me what your mom did to you?" And then I left.

## 4.4 A Family Pattern

My dad couldn't see that he had followed in the footsteps of the very person who caused him so much pain, his mom. I guess he was too close to it. Their relationship had always been stormy. As a young child, I witnessed numerous fights in which they screamed, swore, called each other names, and then parted ways for years at a time. During their separations, his mom would remove him from her will. It was her way of legally divorcing him.

Inevitably, they would patch things up and it would be calm for a while, until something triggered another episode. I felt sorry for my dad when it came to his mom. In her later years, they did make some progress in their relationship, and we saw her and Lloyd more often. Lloyd, her fifth husband, was a very sweet man when he was sober. He liked my dad, encouraged my grandma to maintain the relationship, and when she was angry, made sure my dad stayed in the will.

Not long after Debbie died, my grandma underwent a series of hospitalizations and we all began to wonder how much time she had left. This was particularly concerning because she and my dad were once again not on speaking terms and Lloyd had passed away the year before. No one was there to encourage her to reconcile.

As my parents were getting ready for their annual trip to Mexico, I had a nagging feeling that something could happen to her while they were gone and encouraged my dad to make amends. He took my advice and went to her home. But, when his mom opened the door and saw him, she slammed it in his face. My parents went to Mexico and she died while they were gone.

In the months that followed, my dad became very depressed. Although he refused to get any kind of outside help, he clearly knew the pain of a poor ending. He had experienced it with his own mom.

A few days after his birthday, my dad called me. Despite his initial hostility towards me, my flawed attempt at repairing our relationship must have hit a soft spot. Dad said he was sorry for how he reacted, and then deflected by talking about his mom and all the ways she had failed him growing up. It was confusing. Was he blaming her for how he acted with me? All I could think to say was, "You should have never been treated like that."

My mom would later call the conversation "a miracle" because it is one of the few times, he ever apologized to anyone. It wasn't a complete turnaround, but we were both trying. My dad started coming around and helping us with some home projects. We were slowly remodeling the "smelly" old house and he scraped off popcorn ceilings, painted, and laid tile in the kitchen and bathroom. I knew it was his way of saying he cared about me and I responded by appreciating the effort. I tried to be warmer, more conversational, and make eye contact when I spoke to him, although this was surprisingly difficult. Progress was slow, but the wall I had built was coming down and I began to expect our relationship to end well.

## 4.5 Emotional immaturity

When the church was six years old, I found myself rapidly losing enthusiasm for my job. We had grown to an average weekly attendance of 1200, and the demands on our growing staff team were high. I was putting in about fifty hours a week at the office and also working from home in the evenings.

---

"Some trauma survivors have difficulty regulating emotions such as anger, anxiety, sadness, and shame. This is more so when the trauma occurred at a young age." [15]

---

Fatigued and feeling pressured, my inability to hold it together became a big problem. Being a female leader on a predominately male staff was a challenge. Many times, there was unexpected resistance to my coaching. I also encountered conflict from others in the church, when making unpopular decisions. A conflict avoider my whole life, I quickly learned skills that helped me approach these conversations in a healthier way. However, the rejection was painful, and I wore my feelings on my sleeve. As a result, people around me observed my many emotional ups and downs. This was hard on my staff team. I was their coach and needed to create a sense of stability, not add drama.

My Senior Pastor was the initial one to flag this as a problem. In a yearly evaluation, he said, "Your emotional immaturity is holding back your leadership potential." I was shocked. I knew I was sensitive, but the label "emotional immaturity" took me by surprise. I was deeply embarrassed and wanted to quit.

Thankfully, my husband, Lynn and Jillian convinced me there was hope. I stayed in my role and made an all-out effort to change. I bought books on emotional intelligence, took surveys, and mustered up all the self-control I could. Much to my dismay, I did not make one iota of progress! In fact, it's possible my condition actually worsened.

## 4.6 Tea-Time

My fragile emotions became an obstacle outside the workplace as well. I had been a part of a weekly women's get-together for years. By design it was very informal. Five of us met weekly at a coffee shop to share life events and exchange prayer requests. However, when the group decided to change the format and study a book on sexual intimacy, I opted out! The book was well written and highly respected, but I had a visceral reaction to the content and conversation. I didn't want to talk about sex or intimacy. Years later, I would learn why.

I left that group and started another one with Lynn and Jillian. Every week the three of us met at a tea shop to support each other and pray.

By this time, Jillian and I had become very close. For several years, we spent time together weekly praying for staff and church members. When she got married and left our church, we continued our relationship with frequent phone calls and occasional coffee dates. I didn't know her new husband Jacob very well, but Jillian described him as her prince charming. I was happy for my friend, who had spent many years working full-time as a single mom. In many ways, being a homemaker was her dream come true.

Jacob owned and managed a small farm he inherited from his parents, and worked part-time for the school district as a custodian. The farmhouse was old, and they began a remodel project soon after marrying. However, this quickly became a source of dissatisfaction for Jillian. Jacob was slow, laid back, and lacked initiative. Although he planned to do a lot of the work on the house himself, as time passed, it became obvious his timeline was quite different than Jillian's. Consequently, my joy-filled, enthusiastic friend changed. She began to complain about her husband to me on a regular basis, and I felt like I was back in high school, listening to my mom at the kitchen counter. She talked, I listened, and then encouraged her to get counseling. But she never did. I hoped the new group would help her.

We met very early in the mornings so that Lynn could attend. Lynn and I had developed a very strong friendship. Because her husband Paul attended the church's leadership development program, I also saw him on a regular basis. Initially I found Paul to be very compassionate and an inspiring leader. He had big dreams for helping the needy and financially investing in faith-based nonprofits.

But the more time I spent with Paul the more obvious it became that he was a very complicated man whose emotions fluctuated wildly. When he was up, he was excited, enthusiastic, and filled with creativity. But when he was down, he had problems with anger, depression, and relationships.

Over time, although Lynn was cautious with what she shared, I was aware she and Paul were experiencing ongoing marital problems. I listened, and sometimes asked questions, but Lynn was reluctant to give details, often citing she didn't want to disrespect Paul.

Jillian and Lynn didn't know each other very well when we first started our tea-shop get-togethers, but before long, we were like the three musketeers! We met weekly, talked on the phone regularly, and as a result, our friendships continued to deepen. We didn't know it then, but soon our lives and struggles would be intertwined in unimaginable ways.

## 4.7 Roots of Rejection

Another year passed, and my yearly evaluation rolled around. Although glowing in many respects, my "emotional immaturity" was once again flagged as a problem. My Senior Pastor suggested I consider enlisting the help of a counselor. Very intuitively he speculated, "I just wonder if there is something you haven't dealt with in your past."

I drove home that night in tears and immediately called Lynn. I couldn't imagine continuing in my job. I felt so humiliated, embarrassed, and defeated at my lack of progress. To be honest, my inability to control my emotions began to be a source of self-hatred. I couldn't seem to climb out of the pit I was in. (Even though I read *Get Out of that Pit* by Beth Moore three times!)

Lynn, who was the queen of emotional self-control, encouraged me to get some outside help and wait. She didn't want me to make an emotional decision I would later regret. I knew she was right. I am not sure why counseling seemed to be such a last-ditch effort for me. After all those years spent trying to convince my mom to try it, why hadn't I considered it sooner? Was I reluctant to expose my weaknesses, concerned about the cost, or afraid of what I would discover? I honestly didn't know. What I did know, is that I was finally at the end of my rope. I started to pray about who to see, and not long after, met a woman whose husband had a counseling practice. Upon further investigation, I decided to make an appointment with him.

I was pretty nervous on my first visit to see Walter. However, he was a very sensitive, gentle man who put me at ease almost immediately.

After explaining my problems with emotional immaturity, Walter took some time to describe his approach to counseling. We would be praying together, relying on the Holy Spirit to lead and guide our time together.

Comfortable with what he was offering, we began a session on reflection, and immediately an image of a heart with a network of roots surrounding it surfaced in my mind along with the words: "roots of rejection." When we explored what those roots of rejection might be, surprisingly what came to mind was not the recent experiences at the church, but something that happened when I was in high school. This was very frustrating to me. I was now in my forties, wasn't it time to move on? Yet, as I recalled the memory, even though twenty-five years had passed, a lump formed in my throat and tears stung my eyes. I wondered why it still hurt.

---

"Where a person is OVERREACTING, is probably a place where they are being triggered and the mind is activating painful emotions rooted in former unresolved conflict of past memories." [16]

---

The memory was of an assault that happened at my dad's restaurant the summer before my junior year of high school. I was scheduled to be the opening waitress, which meant I started my shift at four am. The cook arrived at the same time, and once inside, the two of us started prepping for the breakfast rush. Meanwhile, every day like clockwork, a group of older farmers came in to drink coffee and visit.

On this particular day, while I was getting the group of regulars seated, one of them cornered me. He was an unassuming older man, with a big cowboy hat and even bigger belly. I wasn't sure what was happening, as he came closer and closer, eventually pinning me up against the wall. Then, with his back to the rest of the group, he began fondling my breasts!! My hands were full. I had coffee cups in one hand, and a full pot of coffee in the other, which limited my ability to push him away. Why didn't I pour the hot pot of coffee all over him and tell him to leave me alone? Was I shocked? Ashamed? Both?

I tried to avoid him on subsequent mornings, but to no avail. He assaulted me again in the same manner a few days later. Humiliated and afraid, I decided to tell my dad. I was fully expecting him to go ballistic and beat the guy up. Much to my surprise, my dad didn't get angry. Instead, he laughed hysterically. Equally as painful, my mom who was sitting next to him didn't say a word.

---

"Offenders protect and defend other offenders, including those who abused them." *[17]*

---

After recounting the incident to Walter, he led me into visualizing how this experience affected me. I saw a flood rising, a flood of hurt. We continued the session, this time with the intent to take that "flood of hurt" I was carrying and give it to Jesus. Walter asked me if I would picture Jesus on the cross, looking down at me. As I did, he said, "Ok, now picture yourself giving Jesus that flood of hurt." With my eyes closed, I tried to imagine Jesus, stretched out on the cross, turning his head towards me as I approached Him with my pain.

Suddenly, I opened my eyes, sat up in my chair, and said, "I could never do that!" I was surprised by my reaction, but I honestly couldn't imagine inflicting more pain onto my Savior. Apparently, I was comfortable with the idea of Jesus carrying my sins, but not my shame, pain or my sorrow.

We went back into prayer, and this time I did give Jesus the pain of that experience, and in return I saw Him smile and give me a flower. It was a daisy, a spring flower that made me think of new life.

My sessions with Walter continued for several months until we agreed I now had the needed tools to work through any emotional struggles that surfaced on my own. If I was overreacting to a situation, there was likely a reason why. I needed to go to Jesus, ask for revelation, and then respond accordingly.

In the coming months, I began to use my "new tools" on a regular basis and saw significant changes in my emotional control as a result. I was in awe! God's resurrection power was doing what I had been unable to do on my own. I believed I was turning a new corner. In fact, I'm quite sure I thought I was done recovering from my childhood.

## 4.8 The Sky Darkens

Two years passed and while on a visit to see Mike and me, my parents reported my dad had received some bad news from the doctor. The medication used to treat his anemia had stopped being effective. The disease was advancing, and he had been given less than two years to live.

Later that evening, while in the kitchen washing dishes, I wondered why I wasn't more upset about the news. Then I had a very vivid thought, one of those that you just don't forget: "Well, our relationship isn't what I hoped it would be, but it's not ending all that bad either." Little did I know how very wrong I would be! My dad went on to live another eight years, and for most of that time, he considered me his enemy.

---

**TRIGGERING EVENTS**

Delayed onset PTSD can be triggered by many things. The more common triggering events that survivors of sexual abuse experience are listed below: [18]

1. Unknowingly experiencing a situation that is similar in some way to the original issue. This is the most common trigger, but it is usually not understood until after the abuse memories have been retrieved.
2. Death of a sexually abusive perpetrator or the death of a parent you are unconsciously protecting from knowledge of the abuse.
3. Pregnancy or birth of a child or grandchild.
4. A child you identify with reaching the age at which you were abused.

5. Entering a new developmental stage, such as puberty or middle age.

6. Confronting a known sexual abuser. The aftermath of such a confrontation is often the return of memories of abuse by another perpetrator or memories of more severe abuse by the recently confronted perpetrator.

7. Ending an addiction. The addiction to drugs, alcohol, food, gambling or sex has served to stop the memories from emerging and has medicated the pain caused by the abuse. Without the anesthetizing addiction, memories emerge.

8. Intrusion of the reality of sexual abuse. This can occur through media, as in a TV special or newspaper story about sexual abuse, or a friend or relative disclosing that they were sexually abused.

9. Feeling safe. You are in a situation where you feel secure enough to finally face the abuse...

10. Feeling strong. Personal growth leaves you strong enough to face what could not be faced before....

---

# Lynn
## Behind Closed Doors—Losing my Voice

When I met Laurel, I was in a new house, new church, new city, without close friends. Laurel's ability to sense God's direction and her willingness to follow Him challenged me. I was eager to spend as much time with her as possible. I knew Jillian by reputation as a woman of prayer and welcomed the invitation to join their group.

Relationships have always been a high value for me. I moved only one time during my childhood, at age four. I graduated from high school with many of the same friends I started kindergarten with. This stability allowed me to develop long-lasting relationships through young adulthood.

Stability is also a word that describes my parents. I was adored as a child and grew up in a loving Christian home. My parents were safe people who encouraged my sister and me to be ourselves. I never had any trouble speaking up and sharing my feelings but was always encouraged to do so.

I recall one time as a teenager, I needed a pair of shoes for church. Mom took me to several local shoe stores, but I could not find a single pair. When my grandparents came for a visit, we all piled in the car to do some sightseeing in LA. Dad noticed a street lined with shoe stores and encouraged my mom and me to get out and shop. He was confident I would succeed with all those options. He circled the large city block in traffic several times with my grandparents in the back seat until my mom and I returned to the car without any shoes! No one got upset or questioned my lack of decisiveness. The next week, my mom patiently took me to yet another mall and I finally made a choice.

The freedom to speak my mind and share my heart began to change as a result of my relationship with Paul. When Paul and I met, I was casually dating three guys, working in a restaurant, and active in the college group at church. Paul swept me off my feet, and before long the other guys weren't in the picture. He knew what he wanted, and it was me! He was handsome and energetic, and I enjoyed being the object of his attention.

---

"Abusers will mask their abusive behavioral patterns while dating. They will be on their best behavior. I encourage women to wait two years before marrying for this reason." Dr. Mary Dietzen

---

After nine months, we were engaged, and we married shortly after dating for just a year. Part of the sense of urgency was sexual attraction and the difficulty in waiting for marriage. My parents weren't too excited about it. They asked us to wait, they had some reservations.

One concern was about Paul's dishonesty. Early in our relationship, they discovered he had greatly exaggerated his college football success. He had in fact gone to a community college instead of Washington State

*University. When confronted with this lie, he confessed that he wanted to impress us, and seemed contrite. I quickly forgave, but my parents weren't as quick to forget. But they chose not to oppose our marriage when it was clear we weren't open to waiting.*

*My best friend from childhood had her own reservations. She agreed to be my matron of honor, but later, our friendship became awkward and eventually we stopped spending time together. She would be the first of many relationships I lost because of my relationship with Paul.*

*Paul was romantic and affectionate. He bought me flowers and we had regular date nights. Most of the time I felt loved and appreciated by him. But his emotions were labile. His feelings about me varied widely from to-tal devotion to acute disappointment, and I usually didn't understand what caused the change. My failures included: being late, being disorganized, being negative about change, and being too goody-goody. When he was upset with me, I apologized, and put effort into improving myself. I wanted him to be pleased with me, so I started keeping much of my thoughts and feelings to myself.*

---

"The victim often tries to please the abuser by trying to avoid situations that end in the verbal abuse, but it doesn't stop the next phase of the cycle from happening." [19]

---

*Paul had multiple bouts of depression. One followed the downturn of his building business. The low point came one night when we argued, and I decided to go for a drive to take a breather. He came outside with a rifle, threatening to shoot if I didn't get out of the car, but I was paralyzed with fear in the front seat. He shot into the hood to prevent me from leaving, then took the butt of the rifle and shattered the windshield.*

*Neighbors heard the shots and called 911, police came quickly, and he was arrested. He spent the night in jail, and I told no one. I went to the arraignment the next day, and they let him out that night. I wasn't afraid, just worried for him. We checked him into an inpatient mental health clinic where he stayed for several weeks. Afterwards he pursued outpatient counseling and started dealing with his traumatic childhood. Things seemed better. The violence seemed then, like an isolated incident, now behind us. I did not feel like I was in an abusive situation.*

*One lasting cost of that outburst, however, was the loss of my close friendships with three women from my church. They were hurt and offended that I had kept Paul's arrest a secret. They found out when reading a police blotter in the newspaper of our small town. They didn't openly drop me, but over time our friendships grew distant. This was a repeated pattern in my life that I see now, looking back.*

*We moved about every three years because of Paul's frequent job changes. I expressed reluctance, but when I spoke my mind I would be criticized, so I ended up being supportive of what he wanted to do and kept my feelings quiet. I didn't realize that I was slowly losing my voice.*

---

"Abusive men will have frequent job changes because of behavior issues (anger, lying, womanizing) but will not tell their spouse the real reason for the job change." Dr. Mary Dietzen

---

*In 2001 we made another move, to Spokane. We bought a boat, and spent a happy summer playing on the lake and remodeling our Spokane home. Paul decided our children needed stability and made a commitment to stay. This was a big relief to me, evidence that he had been listening after all.*

*When the violence returned, it really took me by surprise. Almost ten years had passed since that "isolated incident." The trigger seemed to be the teenage years of parenting. Our beautiful eldest daughter Ashley was a typical teenager who freely spoke her mind. One Thanksgiving, during the long drive home from Seattle to Spokane, she was argumentative. Paul stopped the car and dragged her out by her hair. I don't remember what I did, this shames me to admit. Was I paralyzed in the front seat?*

*When we got home, he cried, saying he should leave, but I didn't want him to go. Instead we started counseling again. When he told the counselor what happened, I feared CPS would be contacted. Looking back, I can see he didn't get the consequences he deserved, but things settled back into a routine and I minimized the impact. I didn't tell anyone what happened. Not Laurel, not my parents, no one. I responded like I had ten years earlier.*

*I didn't realize we were caught in the classic cycle of abuse, which would repeat itself. Paul's anger continued to surface periodically over the next several years. His emotions varied widely, and I rode the roller coaster with him. As tension would build at home, I tried to take pressure off him by staying steady and being low maintenance. In response to disappointments at work and with friends, Paul began to drink regularly, coming home late or not at all. I was worried sick when he didn't come home and felt like I was walking on eggshells when he did. I never knew whether he would be happy or angry, or what might set him off. I certainly didn't speak my mind and share my heart; it wasn't safe.*

---

"Domestic Violence Pattern:
1. Violent incident occurs
2. Offender blames and silences his wife and children
3. No one talks about it
4. Honeymoon phase
5. Stress and tension starts building until the next incident."
   Dr. Mary Dietzen

---

*But my daughter Ashley did speak out. She would stand up to him. Sometimes he responded well, and other times he didn't. He struck her face and left a bruise one time. I kept her home from school the next day. Again, I feared CPS involvement.*

After Paul's angry outbursts, his tension was released, and he always apologized. He told us how much he loved us. His father was angry and abusive, and he verbalized his desire to not repeat the same mistakes. This phase of reconciliation was followed by a period of calm. Paul could be very loving towards me and the kids. He was often the fun one, spontaneous and energetic.

One anniversary, he surprised me with a beautiful canvas print of a two-story house, and a woman kneeling in front of a heart-shaped pond feeding swans. There were more than twenty-five hearts hidden in the picture. That fall he improved a small pond in our front yard to incorporate a dramatic water feature and shaped the pond into a heart to match the picture. I felt loved by his extravagant gifts. These honeymoon periods gave me hope. I did not see they were just a part of the cycle to be followed by building tension and another eventual outburst, repeated indefinitely.

While I kept my heart guarded and my mouth closed at home, I opened up at church. Laurel saw abilities in me to teach and lead that I could not see in myself. After attending for a year, she asked me to take over as the Women's Ministry leader. We met often so she could coach me in my new role. I found that I enjoyed most aspects of teaching and loved interacting with women. Unlike at home, I was appreciated for sharing my thoughts, insights, and opinions.

Unfortunately, my involvement and affirmation at church caused increased tension in our marriage. Paul felt the church valued me and my gifts over him and his. He began to complain about the amount of time I spent volunteering. When the church decided to change my volunteer position to a paid one, he berated me for working for minimum wage. He accused me of caring more about the people at church than him. His growing unhappiness with my ministry role caused great anxiety. I didn't want to displease him, and I didn't believe I should serve in the church without the support of my husband.

During that time God began to prompt me to speak my mind and share my heart with Paul. I shared honestly that I felt I was in my sweet-spot leading Women's Ministry. I prayed that God would change his attitude and asked Paul to support me. Instead, he became relentless in his op-position. Eventually, I shared about this tension with Laurel and told her I wasn't sure if I could continue. Afterwards, Paul confused me by telling me I was overreacting–he said if I quit it was totally my choice and he didn't want to be blamed for it! So, I continued, and his opposition continued as well.

Ultimately, I gave up Women's ministry and went to work for Paul in our home-based construction business. I felt if I did what Paul wanted then he wouldn't be able to blame me anymore. It was a big loss, followed by a sea-son of grief. My heart's desire to serve my husband, my family and God at the same time was a broken dream.

---

"Abusers insecurities increase as their victim's confidence in-creases. Instead of being proud, they are jealous of accomplish-ments" Dr. Mary Dietzen

---

One key friendship that did not suffer when I stepped down from min-istry was mine with Laurel. She continued to spend time with me; we would often go for walks in the neighborhood and I would share my feelings of sadness and loss. However, I continued the pattern of keeping Paul's alco-hol use and physical violence a secret from Laurel and other friends.

 **Jillian**

## Behind Closed Doors—To Share or Not to Share

I was slightly nervous as I drove to our first tea shop meeting. There were some problems surfacing in my marriage that I hadn't been able to admit to anyone, not even Laurel. Jacob was having trouble with intimacy. Proud of the fact he had saved himself for our wedding night, he often made me feel special by saying he had waited his whole life for me. It never crossed my mind that by his forties, the fact he was a virgin might be a *problem.*

*This was my third marriage. Twice divorced, my first marriage lasted nine years, and my second less than two. I married my high school sweetheart two months after graduation, and we had one child. We were both immature and didn't know how to tackle the difficult circumstances that arose in our marriage. When it ended, I put on a brave face, and pushed myself forward without processing my mistakes.*

*I was single for a year when fate brought me into contact with my second husband. A misdialed phone call connected us. He was the boy next door when we were kids and the first boy I ever kissed. This fit into my fairytale idea of romance. What could possibly go wrong with a history like that? The high school love I had trusted broke my heart. Surely a childhood sweetheart was going to be my happily-ever-after.*

---

"There is no such thing as a knight in shining armor. If it seems too good to be true it probably is." Dr. Mary Dietzen

---

*But this marriage quickly became verbally abusive shortly after the birth of our daughter. I tried to keep the peace at all costs, leaning on codependent habits I learned at a young age. Soon the abuse escalated to physical. To help me cope with the chaos, I went to counseling. There, I identified some unhelpful patterns and gained the strength to stand up to him. After a separation and a failed attempt at reconciling, we divorced. I wished I had had the strength and tools to have done so sooner.*

*The next thirteen years of my life were consumed with being a single mom to my two children. It was difficult to make ends meet and provide a stable home for my kids. I worked hard, sometimes holding down several jobs at one time. My struggles made me aware of my need for God. I saw Him provide in answer to my prayers, and my faith grew by leaps and bounds as a result. Attending church regularly and building healthy friendships contributed to that growth.*

*Although I dated when the opportunity presented itself, my kids and my job consumed most of my time and energy. I prayed often about a life partner, and at times felt God reassure me that one day I would remarry. By the time my kids were grown, the longing to be married became stronger.*

*I met Jacob at a concert. He was tall, handsome, and took an immediate interest in me. He was thoughtful and kind. I was really impressed that he even brought his Bible to some of our dates. Most of these dates consisted of long talks in parks and scenic drives. There were great conversations about our faith in God, and how our lives seemed to be heading down the same path.*

*But we also had our differences. Jacob was very frugal. I had seen God's ability to supply all my needs and lacked the worry he had about having enough money for the future. Jacob's upbringing by older parents taught him to hold tight to everything, including all the family "heirlooms" left behind. The rooms in his house were rather full.*

*Although my pastor expressed some reservations and concerns about our relationship, we were married ten months later. After a rough start with sex on our honeymoon, I thought we were adjusting well. But Jacob started having trouble getting excited. He would tell me he needed to close his eyes and visualize me being naked in order to perform. This led me to believe I wasn't pretty enough or sexy enough. He wasn't happy with the real me and had to resort to a mind visual of perhaps a skinnier-and-in-better-shape me just to make love.*

---

"When you don't experience unconditional love as a child, you have a propensity to put up with dysfunctional behavior. Your bar is too low." Dr. Mary Dietzen

---

*Jacob reassured me the problem was him and not me, but his visualizations continued. It was the only way we could be intimate. I started getting worried that something was wrong with him medically. He finally*

*agreed to get a checkup. The doctor couldn't find any medical reason for his impotence and gave him a prescription to help him perform. It seemed to help a little. I still longed for him to connect with me and asked him to keep his eyes open during intimacy. He did so to appease me, but they were glazed over as if he was staring at something in his mind. He definitely wasn't connecting with me.*

*I'm normally a sound sleeper but one night something woke me up at 2:15am. I rolled over to snuggle up to Jacob. My outstretched arm habitually fell across his bare shoulder, but this time it landed on his empty side of the bed. Perhaps he couldn't sleep either. I got up and made my way into the living room. He was sprawled out on the couch naked watching TV.*

*I asked if he was ok. He said yes, he just couldn't sleep. I sat there with him a couple of minutes then asked him to come back to bed. I didn't get married to sleep alone! He reluctantly got up and walked with me down the hall to the bedroom. I tried to cuddle up next to him, but he said he was too hot. I had a hard time falling back to sleep. I was bothered by something, but I couldn't figure out what it was. I stared at the clock while I listened to his rhythmic snoring. Sometime after five a.m. I finally fell back to sleep.*

---

"Although you may not know what is wrong, your gut feeling is right 100% of the time. Don't ignore your intuition. Find out more. Ask more questions." Dr. Mary Dietzen

---

*The excuses started increasing as to why he didn't want sex. He was too tired, he had too much gas, he had a headache, he didn't feel well, or hadn't showered. Eventually he started saying he was just getting old and his testosterone levels were going down (in spite of the fact the doctor said they were normal). I was hurt and felt the sting of rejection. I wasn't good enough. If there was nothing wrong with him, it must be me.*

*To bury the pain, I started focusing less on our intimate relationship*

*and more on our remodel project that still wasn't done. I was losing the battle in the bedroom; since I couldn't fix that, I would jump to the next thing. Somehow, I had to regain control. But there was a similar lack of momentum in this area as well. I would make lists, draw up budgets, shop for deals, and pick out supplies. Jacob would verbalize agreement with the plans. But when it came down to actually doing the work, there was always a "reason" why he couldn't start.*

*I complained a lot during my conversations with Laurel. I was beyond frustrated that we weren't making any progress with the house. My unhappiness grew. Venting my frustration about Jacob was one way of venting the pain of rejection in the bedroom without having to address it. I was stuck in a vicious cycle. I believed Jacob when he said he shared my goals, but I failed to see that his actions were speaking louder than his words.*

*These false starts and abrupt let-downs were becoming a pattern. A few years later, I discovered what turned out to be the tip of the iceberg...*

# 5

# Ashamed

The clock struck midnight. In a **panic** Cinderella **ran,** ashamed and afraid the prince would discover the truth about her identity. She was a victim; mistreated and **abused** by those who were supposed to love and cherish her. In her haste, she left behind one glass slipper on the palace steps.

## 5.1 Layers

My healing occurred one layer at a time, at a pace I could handle. Forgiving my dad for the emotional and verbal abuse had been the first layer. Identifying and letting go of the pain rooted in rejection had been the second layer.

The third layer was exposed when my senior pastor and his wife decided to take active steps to hire and promote someone to lead alongside him as an executive pastor. I knew he needed this position filled. Even though I had worked closely with him through the years, I felt God had told me someone else would get the promotion. He had other plans for me.

It was disappointing news, but I tried to put on my big-girl pants! After a search that took years, Stan was hired out of California. Although he was not given the executive role right away, I felt it was only a matter of time. This became apparent when I was asked to move out of my private office and give it to him.

Stan was an obvious fit for the role. He had been on a church staff for many years and had excellent credentials. His people skills were off the charts too. From the get-go, everyone liked him; he was fun, kind, and had a great sense of humor. Eventually I began to describe him as the nicest guy in the world. And I meant it.

## 5.2 Escalating Emotional Problems

For many months, Stan and I held equally supportive roles to the senior pastor. This was stressful, more stressful than if he just got promoted over me. Gradually, a myriad of symptoms surfaced as a result. I prayed, applying the tools Walter had given me during my previous round of counseling. This time, I saw no improvement. In fact, my symptoms worsened. What were they?

---

"PTSD (Post-Traumatic Stress Disorder) is a diagnosis used by professionals in the mental health field to describe adverse reactions to severe trauma, including the trauma of sexual abuse." [20]

---

**Anxiety**

I was very anxious. It was like being on heightened alert. I began many days, dreading the future and filled with fear. But I wasn't sure why. I brought this fear into my relationship with God and often felt like I was in trouble. I knew it was not rational, yet my feelings seemed to betray me.

Another change that took place, was equally confusing. Whenever God's love for me was verbalized, I had a visceral reaction, as if someone ran their fingernails against a chalkboard. My heart cried out silently to myself, I couldn't understand why I was struggling with whether God loved me. Intellectually, I knew that He loved me. I knew my feelings were untrue. Why was I feeling this way? Just a few years before, in the same job, I felt His love deeply.

**Depression**

My inability to conquer my anxiety grew and depression followed. I cried easily and often. I was filled with self-contempt. At times I even contemplated suicide. Oddly enough, those thoughts were most predominant during intimacy with my husband. Although I loved Mike and we were not in any disharmony, when together sexually I found myself increasingly uncomfortable.

I didn't hide my dilemma from my friends Lynn and Jillian, not that I could have even if I wanted to. My emotions continued to dominate my moods and speech. So many times, I wished I could be like Lynn, always composed, even when life was throwing her one curve ball after another. Case in point, when Paul's jealousy over her growing popularity and effectiveness as a leader at the church resulted in her resignation, she took it like a trooper. I never saw her cry about it, although I knew she was disappointed.

**Trouble Sleeping**

In addition to the anxiety and depression, I had trouble sleeping. It wasn't uncommon for me to wake up at two or three a.m. and experience insomnia. I also experienced strange dreams that I often could describe in detail after I woke up.

I always processed these kinds of dreams with my friends. They understood how troubling they could be, because at times they experienced vivid dreams too. Sometimes I told my husband, who often responded, "Maybe it's something you ate; what did you have for dinner last night?" Thank God for girlfriends.

---

"PTSD symptoms may start within one month of a traumatic event, but sometimes symptoms may not appear until years after the event. These symptoms cause significant problems in social or work situations and in relationships. They can also interfere with your ability to go about your normal daily tasks." [21]

---

Just as an example, one of the dreams involved my mom and me. In the dream, she was very concerned I was not going to be ready for an upcoming formal dance. At her insistence, I sat down in front of a mirror, ready to have my hair done. Suddenly, I noticed a large tumor on my neck. A friend arrived, and we went to a house. Once inside, I discovered there were many hidden doors. Each door led into a room I didn't know existed. Months later, I realized the tumor was likely a "pain in my neck." The doors and rooms referenced my subconsciousness and the repressed memories I explored in counseling.

Most of the vivid dreams like this one, contained information that supported or aided my recovery in some way. For this reason, I faithfully recorded them in my journals and prayed about them. Over time, God gave me insights about my healing as a result.

## 5.3 Triggers

The escalating anxiety, depression, and insomnia varied in intensity. Some days they were overwhelming, other times I hardly noticed them. It was as if the symptoms were like a scab on a wound that was not completely healed. If that scab was left alone, I was rather stable. However, if circumstances, people, or events touched that scab in any way, I would hemorrhage emotionally. I overreacted.

I've since heard this phenomenon referred to as a "trigger." Triggers are external events or circumstances that may produce very uncomfortable emotional or psychiatric symptoms, such as anxiety, panic, discouragement, despair, or negative self-talk.[22]

What event or circumstance triggered my symptoms? The changes in my job and relationships at the church. Somehow, God orchestrated a replay of what happened to me as a child by mimicking some of the circumstances in my family. However, this replay involved healthy, loving people who were safe. I was not actually in any harm, it just felt like it, which was confusing.

**Panic**

I put up with my escalating emotional problems for months hoping they would resolve with prayer. Then, one day, I had a panic attack. It seemed to come out of nowhere. The morning it occurred, I was in a meeting with Stan, the Senior Pastor, and his wife. These coworkers had become like family to me. It turns out, the "like family" was actually a problem and served to trigger what happened next.

We sat down like we usually did every week to discuss vision, overall strategy, and staffing. I attempted to focus on the agenda in front of me but, for some reason, I couldn't. The room started to seem small. Too small. I looked around for the door and then at the clock. My heart began to race, and over and over my predominant thought was, "I have to get out of here."

Somehow, I restrained myself from running, and after the meeting, lingered behind to describe what happened to my boss. He suspected I had suffered an anxiety attack. Our conversation prompted me to make an appointment with my counselor. I wasn't eager to go back; I think maybe if a root canal would have done the trick, I would have opted for one of those instead! But I knew that counseling had helped in the past, and it would probably be the thing to help me now.

## 5.4 Rescue Plan

Leading up to my appointment with the counselor, I had a number of very strong impressions from the Holy Spirit. They became like bread crumbs leading me down the path I would later learn ended in past sexual abuse.

One of those impressions came the morning of my panic attack. My Bible reading that day focused on Lot's escape from Sodom and Gomorrah. It was a story familiar to me. Lot was rescued by angels who guided him out of the sexually immoral city before it was destroyed with fire.

During my prayer time following the Bible reading, the words, "rescue plan" came to mind. What did I need to be rescued from? It was confusing, but I wrote the words down in my journal anyways. Later, after the revelation of sexual abuse, I returned to this journal entry and was able to interpret what God was saying with amazing clarity! God intended to rescue me from the Sodom and Gomorrah that had been my childhood!

## 5.5 Breadcrumbs

The day of my appointment with the counselor arrived. After calling Jillian and getting some prayer over the phone, I went to work. While walking down the hall, I had another strong impression from the Holy Spirit: "I can restore your innocence." What? Why would I need my innocence restored? Instantly, I was reminded of my long-held suspicion that something terrible had happened to me as a child. I thought about my history of repeated childhood nightmares and unexplained phantom physical symptoms (body memory) and decided I would mention them to Walter.

I sat in his office, only a few hours later, and was embarrassed. My symptoms and apparent lack of emotional control was just plain embarrassing to me. But I pressed through, and began to describe the least threatening subject, which was the panic attack. Then, as the appointment neared the end of the hour, I drummed up the courage to ask Walter if there were any significance to repeated childhood dreams.

He said there could be and asked me to describe mine. I told him about the little boy I often dreamt about growing up. He was about five or six with curly blond hair. Every time I saw him in my dreams, he always did the same thing. While sitting on a bale of hay, he lifted his finger up revealing a bloody stump. He looked sad but was not crying or speaking.

We were out of time, and Walter asked if we could pray. As I closed my eyes, an image of a baseball bat being swung and coming straight towards my head came to mind along with the words, "A big blow." Immediately afterwards, an image of a man's penis appeared.

More breadcrumbs. I left the office with a pretty good idea where this was all headed—I had been sexually abused. The question was no longer "If," but "Who?"

## 5.6 Midnight

I went to my next appointment with Walter, terrified and pensive. I believed something had happened, but who did it? The most likely person in my mind was my uncle Steve, my dad's stepbrother. After all, he had attempted to talk me into engaging in a sexual act with him when I was in elementary school.

I spent the hour with Walter unable to recall anything from my childhood. It was a total waste of time, money, and emotional energy. Was this going to work? Walter must have read my mind and asked me to consider bringing a girlfriend to my next appointment.

# Lynn:

*Laurel asked me to accompany her to a counseling appointment, and I readily agreed. She explained that she was having trouble making progress with Walter, and he thought bringing a safe female friend might help. Laurel might, on some subconscious level, feel reluctant to open-up freely to a man. I could understand that, having difficulty myself opening-up to Paul.*

*Laurel and I were close friends; I shared with her more than anyone else what was going on in my life. She had supported me through the turmoil of leaving Women's Ministry and had continued in our friendship even though we no longer worked together. We talked often about her struggles at work, and I wanted to support her in any way I could.*

*We were both a little nervous sitting in the waiting area of Walter's office. When he invited us in, I remember thinking his office was different than any other counselor I had seen. It was roomy, almost home-like and child-friendly. There were pencil drawings on the walls of lambs and Jesus.*

*Walter gave me an assignment, which instantly increased my nervousness. He handed me a legal pad and a pen. While he talked with Laurel I was to concentrate and write down anything that came to mind. This was not what I had expected. What if I didn't hear anything? Would I ruin the experience for Laurel?*

*I concentrated on my assignment, worried I would mess it up, while Walter guided Laurel through some visualization. She was recalling an incident from her childhood. She told Walter what she saw, that as a toddler, she was in the front seat of a truck with her dad. The only thing that came to mind for me was, "It's not your fault," so I wrote it down. I strained to try to hear something else, but I wasn't any good at it and nothing else came to the surface of my mind.*

*Then Laurel started recalling more, became audibly upset, and spoke only in phrases. She continued to talk about the images she was seeing. She mentioned a lollipop, and then gasped and cried out, "What kind of girl does that?" I wasn't exactly sure what she had seen, but knew it was connected with a very disturbing memory with her father and could guess about the context.*

*Walter continued to speak with Laurel gently and led her through prayer about what she had seen. Then he turned to me and asked me if I heard anything. Laurel was weeping, and I choked up as I said the only thing I had written, over and over again on the legal pad: "It's not your fault. It's not your fault. It's not your fault. It's not your fault. It's not your fault!"*

From that day forward, I described recalling the memory of what took place in that truck with my dad as my "midnight" experience. It was pivotal to my story. Just like midnight marks both the end of one day and the beginning of another, my "midnight" did the same thing. It changed how I defined myself. One day I was a Christian wife, mom, pastor, and friend. The next day, my whole identity was wrapped up in being a victim of incest! I felt dirty, and ashamed. I wanted to run, hide, and never return. I couldn't imagine facing my dad, my mom or anyone else for that matter. My new reality was so awful, I pleaded with God to let me die.

# Lynn

## *Behind Closed Doors—Nothing I Say Matters*

*Six months after leaving women's ministry, Paul took me to dinner and asked me what I wanted to do with my life. He said he wanted to support my dream since I had supported his. I felt lost—what I really wanted to do, I left behind and couldn't get back. Everything had changed with women's ministry and the leadership had been given to someone else.*

*Despite my efforts to help my marriage by giving up my role in women's ministry, things at home got worse instead of better. I prayed, sought God's help, and felt challenged to speak my mind and share my heart. But when I took the risk to share my feelings—whether in private, in counseling or in small group—Paul would withdraw or accuse me of making him the bad guy. I felt terribly lonely. I poured out my thoughts and feelings to God in the pages of my journal; I didn't feel I could tell anyone else. I wrote honestly about Paul's part, but I focused a lot on what was wrong with me. If only I was a stronger person or communicated better.*

---

"In an abusive relationship, victims lose themselves in the relationship and give up their identity for the other person. In a healthy relationship, both people have separate identities, interests, and activities. They take turns making sacrifices for the other person." Dr. Mary Dietzen

---

*Paul attended a ministry training institute at our church and dreamed of creating a business with a mission. He wanted to invest in the lives of employees and give the profits to missions in Africa. Several other Christian men caught his vision and they started a construction company together. They prayed, read the Bible together, and sought to run the business like a ministry. The office was housed in a shop on our property; my commute to work was a short walk across the driveway.*

*One afternoon, Paul called to say the county was making us move our business because our next-door neighbors had complained. We were shocked; we never thought we were doing anything wrong. I told Paul to wait to talk to our neighbors about the conflict until I could go with him.*

*However, after a few beers, he headed across the street spewing hatred and verbally assaulting both husband and wife while they were outside in their front yard. I didn't witness the altercation. I was on the phone but could hear loud yelling and quickly made an excuse to hang up. I was so upset that he would declare war on our neighbors and argued with him in front of the girls. He raged back at me and flipped me off.*

*I asked him to come outside and talk. I spoke my mind calmly, telling him that this raging and swearing was not the man I knew him to be. He accused me of emasculating him. I disagreed and told him that he was becoming violent. Eventually he calmed down and we made peace.*

*The conflict with our neighbors weighed heavily on me. Since Paul wasn't ready to apologize, I attempted to talk with the wife the next day on the phone. While discussing what happened, Paul called repeatedly. I cut off the conversation with her, without coming to any resolution when he called the fourth time. He was intensely angry that I hadn't stopped what I was doing and taken his call. I apologized but said no more.*

*Paul didn't come home until 1:30am that night. I didn't know where he was, or what he was doing. Our son was frantic for him—crying and couldn't sleep because he wanted Daddy. I wanted to be angry at Paul, but I actually felt little emotion when he finally came home. He had been drinking and he wanted to talk. He wouldn't just go to bed. He told me he understood if I wanted out. I kept quiet; I didn't care to engage him in a conversation that might end poorly. But I felt that even if I left, I could not escape. My kids still needed their dad, and I could not make up for his absence, not even for one evening.*

*When Paul woke up the next morning, he was sorry and wanted to talk; I was hurt and angry. I was able to express to him that we were walking different paths, but I had not changed my direction—he had. I said that I felt like a failure to him because my love, strong though imperfect, had not made a difference in his life. I shared my thoughts about being wrong for him—how maybe someday he might work through these issues with a stronger, more direct woman. I cried about how our son needed him.*

---

"Honeymoon phase: After an episode of abuse the abuser tries to minimize the episode, and often apologizes and attempts to convince his victim that it will never happen again. He is loving and kind during this phase, and appears to be making a concise effort to not abuse his victim again. Maybe he is making an effort, but it's not long before the cycle starts over." [23]

---

*Paul broke. He cried and held onto me. He told me how bad he wanted to change. I asked him to pray, and he cried out for forgiveness, admitting he'd been a fool and walked away from God. I told him he needed a plan and that if his business was going the wrong direction he would get moving and make a plan to fix it. I told him that he needed to do the same with his life. I said he couldn't run to alcohol anymore. I basically said all that I had in my heart and he listened. Paul said his eyes and ears were opened and he would do whatever it took to change.*

*Friends came over and Paul shared his battle with alcohol, anger, resentment and bitterness. He shared how he'd walked away from God. We all talked, and they prayed for us. We felt it was the start of accountability. I went from the point of giving up to a place of hope. A wall had been broken down between Paul and me, and I felt closer to him than I had in months.*

*But within two short weeks I came home from Costco to Paul demeaning Caleb. I stood up to him—told him in front of the kids that he was not to treat them—any of them—harshly. He had ripped Caleb's new school shirt in his rage. I sent the kids outside and told Paul we would leave until he was ready to apologize.*

*Surprisingly, the kids didn't want to leave. Caleb came back inside, and Paul told me to let him stay. They both sat on the couch watching TV and eventually the girls joined them. Paul never did own up to his actions.*

*I began to realize that nothing I said, however I said it, mattered. Even when I did stand up, it didn't change anything. My efforts to speak my mind and share my heart were futile.*

---

"His abuse is out of her control. As the tension builds, something is going to set him off into an abusive episode. Period." [24]

---

# 6

# Supported

As soon as the coach passed through the palace gates, the magical dress was gone. Cinderella looked down at her raggedy dress, and suddenly noticed that *not everything* was as it was before! The fairy godmother had left **a gift**, a glass slipper, reminding her of the prince's love! She longed to be back in his arms and felt overwhelming **sorrow and loss.** It was over. Her dream had died.

Penniless, and with nowhere else to go, Cinderella chose to return to her old life of servitude and abuse. But thankfully, she was **not alone.** Her friends **stood by her side** and **committed** to be there with her **every step** of the way! Feeling **supported,** Cinderella began to run towards the very place and people that had caused her so much **pain.**

## 6.1 Community is Anesthesia

I left Walter's office and went home. Not long after, I received a text from a good friend of mine. It said: "God's anesthesia for spiritual surgery is community." I knew this nugget of wisdom was born out of her own experience and took it to heart. I then made a conscious choice to be authentic and honest with those in my community about the pain I was in. I decided I wasn't going to hide what I was going through.

As a result, during my recovery, Mike and I had a lot of support. We had a small group of friends from our church that got together each week. It was hard, but I told them I was experiencing PTSD as a result of emerging recollections of being sexually abused as a child. They responded with compassion and acceptance.

I was equally candid with Lynn, Jillian, and another group of girlfriends I met with weekly. During my recovery, these women helped me so much. They listened, got angry, prayed, and cried right along with me.

God also put several women in my life who were survivors of incest, and they mentored me. This was incredibly helpful. I could speak to them about my experience and immediately they "got it." They also imparted valuable wisdom and advice.

Finally, the decision was made to tell the church staff. My coworkers, many of whom were pastors, knew something was wrong. Although I didn't share details with them, I told them I was in the process of recalling some incidents of sexual abuse from my childhood. Most of them didn't want or need to know more than that. But a few came to my office privately and shared their own family histories of sexual abuse. These were people who I respected and viewed as normal, which gave me hope for myself.

## 6.2 Questions

Despite the tremendous emotional support, in the weeks and months following the revelation of abuse, I spiraled emotionally. My next appointment with Walter was over a month away, and in the meantime the questions about my new reality were mounting. I began to write them down and as the list grew, so did my sense that recovery was going to take a very long time.

1. Who can I tell? Should this stay a secret?
2. Am I going crazy?
3. Why go back and dig up the past?
4. Did this really happen?
5. How do I handle all this anger?
6. How much more have I forgotten? How long did it go on?
7. How do I face people?
8. Why do I feel so guilty?
9. Why didn't God protect me?
10. What can I take to relieve the pain?
11. How do I face my dad again?

Initially, I started researching the answers to these questions on my own. I had a one-track mind and became obsessed with figuring out what was going on with me and how to get better. I found several books on repressed memories and healing from sexual abuse and devoured them.

## 6.3 Normalizing My Experience

My insomnia was unmanageable and going to work was getting harder and harder. Every day I put a smile on my face when walking through the office doors, and every day, inevitably someone would show concern and I would end up crying.

One day, while sitting at my desk, with my office door shut, I tearfully started to pray about what to do. Surely God had a solution. As I did, a name floated across my mind: "Janis Bradford." Who was she? I googled the name and discovered there was a counselor named Janis Bradford whose office was less than a mile away from mine. Her specialty was sexual abuse. I picked up the phone and made an appointment for the next day.

Her office was welcoming, the office receptionist warm, but still I was insecure and nervous. What was this counselor going to think about my claims? I tried to picture myself telling her: "So yeah, I just realized when

I was little my dad taught me to give him oral sex...." Was that believable? Was she going to think I was some crazy loony toon?

However, my fears were soon alleviated. Janis was like a breath of fresh air and I immediately felt comfortable with her. As I retold the story of my recent revelation in counseling, Janis was nothing more than supportive, affirming, and concerned. When she asked how I was doing, I was honest and told her I thought often of ending my life. I also expressed I knew I wouldn't; I cared too much about how it would affect my husband and kids. She recommended an antidepressant and reassured me I would get through this. I didn't believe her.

In those first few appointments, as Janis educated me about what I was experiencing and why, I felt some relief. Some of my questions started to be answered and she became a lifeline for me. Soon, Mike started attending my sessions whenever he could as well. We were in this together.

## 6.4 Risking A Friendship

While I was trying to navigate the crisis in my own life, Lynn and Jillian both had challenges of their own. Jillian continued to be very frustrated with Jacob. Her complaints were reasonable. Jacob lacked follow-through, and his expectations were often unreasonable. I'll never forget the time he made her take a box of crackers back to Costco because in his opinion they were "too expensive." The man wanted an account for every penny she spent. Even more concerning to me, was Jillian's compliance. She took the crackers back!

I did my best to listen and be a good friend. Sometimes I challenged her, saying that she seemed intent on changing Jacob. Wasn't he like this when she married him? I recalled how in my early days of being married to Mike, I too focused on his weaknesses instead of my own.

One day Jillian called wanting to talk about Lynn's husband Paul, not Jacob. Lynn was preparing to speak at a Women's Retreat and the leader called Jillian asking for Paul's phone number. She wanted to interview Lynn's husband so she could use his personal reflections of her in the retreat introduction. Jillian didn't know Paul's number, googled it, and incredibly, what appeared was Paul's profile on a dating website!

I was so angry! For some time, Paul's behavior and personality had reminded me of my own dad. His emotional instability, problems with relationships, self-absorption, and unrealistic expectations of Lynn seemed very familiar to me. I knew he had been unfaithful to her early in their marriage, but I thought it was an isolated incident. Clearly, I was wrong.

Jillian wondered what we should do. I didn't wonder, I knew exactly what I was going to do. I was going to tell Lynn. My certainty came as a result of a conversation I once had with my mom. Years had passed, but the memory was vivid. We were in the kitchen of my home, discussing their long-time friends Darrel and Elizabeth. Seemingly out of the blue, my mom said, "Darrel has been unfaithful to Elizabeth for years. He's got a reputation for being quite a lady's man." I was shocked, Darrel seemed like a family man, always happy, kind, and loving towards his wife. I asked my mom, "Does Elizabeth know?" My mom seemed surprised I would ask, and said, "No, I'm sure she doesn't." "Why haven't you told her mom?" I asked. "Because if it was me, I wouldn't' want to know." she said.

This was puzzling and troubling on so many levels. Why would you choose to stay in the dark about a betrayal like that? I never understood this or my mom's lack of disclosure. Her inaction didn't seem consistent with being a good friend to Elizabeth. Faced with a similar situation, I was not going to be guilty of doing the same thing. I knew telling Lynn could risk our friendship, but it was a risk I was willing to take.

I told Jillian I would take care of it and after the retreat, called Lynn. "Hey, I have something serious to discuss with you but wanted to do it in person," I said. She came over later that morning, and we sat on my couch together. I explained that as her friend, I had something difficult to show her. I opened my computer and let her see Paul's dating profile. "I would want you to do the same thing for me if it was Mike," I said.

Lynn didn't say a word. She looked away from the computer screen, then down at the floor, and a long period of silence ensued. Finally, she looked at me very pensively and said, "I can't do this right now." She stood up and walked out my front door without saying another word.

I followed her to the door, watched her get in her car and wondered if our friendship would survive the disclosure.

## 6.5 Paul's Defense

Several days passed. Although I didn't hear from Lynn, I did get a phone call from Paul. His tone was friendly, upbeat, and confident. "Laurel, Lynn showed me the dating profile you discovered. You have to believe me, I never posted that! Someone who has it out for me must have taken that picture and copied it from my Facebook account. They are trying to hurt me and cause me problems. I would never betray Lynn like that!" he said.

I was not surprised by the call, or his defense. The difficulty was knowing how to respond. It didn't seem wise to disagree with him or tell him how unbelievable I found his explanation. Surely this would only alienate Lynn. I thanked Paul for the call and ended the conversation as cordially as I could.

Lynn and I resumed our friendship without discussing it further. However, I was never sorry for speaking the truth to my dear friend. Years later, the subject did resurface, but under the direst of circumstances.

◇◇◇◇◇◇◇◇◇◇◇◇◇◇◇◇◇◇◇◇◇ **Jillian** ◇◇◇◇◇◇◇◇◇◇◇◇◇◇◇◇◇◇◇◇◇

### *Behind Closed Doors—Dismissing a Warning Sign*

*When Monday morning came, I was glad to send Jacob out the door to work. I would have a little time to myself before he got back for his pancake and egg breakfast. I planned on calling my daughter to check on her and "the girls," as I affectionately called my granddaughters. We usually got together once a week and I cherished any time spent with the two of them.*

*I called my daughter; it went to voicemail. This made me feel a little anxious. When we didn't talk, I would start to wonder what I did wrong and think up all kinds of possible, mostly inaccurate, reasons why she hadn't called or returned my call. I was afraid of being rejected. This fear showed up in all my relationships. It was how I normally operated.*

*Before my mind got too carried away with my worst fear, I poured a cup of coffee and sat down at the computer to enter the previous weeks receipts into Quickbooks. Jacob required that I keep a detailed account of every dollar I spent.*

*As I opened the computer, I noticed an unfamiliar picture of a young girl about age eight. It looked like a school photo, taken from the waist up. She had a plaid blouse, blonde hair and a big smile. I was curious why this picture had just been viewed. I'm not very tech savvy, but one thing I had learned was how to right click on the picture to see more details. By doing this, you can see when the picture was last opened and how many times it has been viewed. This smiling little girl's picture had been viewed multiple times. It was last opened at 2:15 a.m. this morning.*

*Questions entered my mind like puzzle pieces. Who was she? Why had her picture been viewed so many times? Why hadn't Jacob mentioned her before when we looked through his family pictures? Since he was a custodian, I thought maybe one of the kids at school gave it to him and he had scanned it into the computer. That still didn't answer the question of why he was up looking at the picture of this little girl at 2:15 a.m.*

*My mind was still trying to figure it all out when Jacob walked in the door from work a short time later. I began asking him questions about the picture of the unknown girl. He answered them honestly and in a matter-of-fact manner.*

*"Is she your relative?" "No," he answered.*

*"Is she a friend's daughter?" "No," he replied.*

*I guessed. "Oh, then she's a student from your school?" Again, came his short reply, "No."*

*"Then who is she?" "Just a girl with a cute smile," he said.*

*My next question to him was, "Why do you have a picture of a little girl you don't know?" As I asked him, I could feel my heart start to beat a little faster. I wondered if it was a secret love child of his, even though he had insisted I was the first girl he had ever been intimate with. "I just thought she was cute," he replied.*

---

"The art of being wise is the art of knowing what to overlook."
William James

---

*I just could not wrap my mind around his answers. Something felt unsettling about it, but I couldn't put my finger on it. Why would a man his age, keep a picture of a little girl that was not a relative? Let alone view it multiple times in the middle of the night? I insisted he delete it. Acting like it was no big deal, he willingly did so. There was an odd feeling in the pit of my stomach. I ignored it, and let logic take over. Since he so willingly deleted it from the computer, I deleted the warning sign from my mind as well. It wasn't till much, much later, that I would be reminded of this.*

*Laurel and I were both growing weary of my dissatisfaction with Jacob. With her encouragement, instead of rehashing and complaining about everything Jacob wasn't doing, I decided to focus on the things Jacob was doing right. Jacob often told me just what I wanted to hear. He said he was proud of me. He was happy to support me in my volunteer activities at his church. He loved having me as his life companion. I determined to focus on how lucky I was that Jacob loved me and wanted me beside him so much. I paid less attention to his lack of action and my gut. I dismissed our conversation about the unknown girl, and as usual, moved on.*

# Lynn
## Behind Closed Doors—Riding the Rollercoaster

*Paul never apologized to our neighbors for his emotional outburst. With the conflict unresolved, he eventually decided we should move. Initially I protested, but he criticized me for not thinking clearly, or speaking up sooner. I felt so run over by his desires that I didn't fight for what I wanted. We moved only a few miles to an extravagant home on a sixteen-acre lavender farm. The kids would stay in the same school, which met my desire for stability. I chose to be satisfied with that.*

*That summer before my oldest daughter Ashley's senior year of high school, we took her on a three-week trip to South Africa. Paul's goal was to invest some of the business profits in a venture that would provide financial support for a missionary friend.*

*I was overwhelmed by the poverty, prejudice, and disparity in living conditions depending on skin color. We drove right past the shanty townships on our way to our oceanfront condo each night, and my stomach was sick with the contrast. We visited people dying of AIDS who lived in cardboard shacks without water or electricity. We prayed for them but had no medications to help ease their symptoms. I was struck by the ocean-sized need, and my impact only the size of a small glass of water.*

*I came home from Africa with a decision to renew my nursing license, so I could go back and volunteer. Ashley came home with a heart to help the disadvantaged, which led her to choose a college major in global development studies. Paul came home with disappointment that his business venture didn't pan out. He continued to pull away from God, which had a ripple effect on how he treated his family.*

*The roller coaster was at high speed now with huge dips and heights of emotion, and I just hung on for dear life. His temper flared towards me and the kids more often. Instead of moving away when he was angry, I moved towards him, trying to make things better, be more pleasing, and keep the peace.*

*One Sunday, we argued over something inconsequential, and he called* all three kids to sit on the couch in the living room. He told them we were getting a divorce. I was shocked. We hadn't ever talked about it. Ashley was quiet. Beth started crying, and Caleb wailed and ran out to the second story deck as if he was going to jump off. I calmed and reassured the kids while Paul retreated to the bedroom.

After such blowups, he would be apologetic. He would express how much I meant to him and how sorry he was for his behavior. Instead of pushing me away, he would want me close. His warmth towards me felt good and would reassure me for a time. But the cycle would inevitably repeat. In order to cope with the repeated rejection, I held onto the good times and minimized the bad. I became numbed to my own feelings; my highs and lows were muted. I was resigned to the reality that I couldn't please my husband.

I became suspicious of repeated cell phone conversations with a female customer. When I confronted both of them separately, they denied any wrongdoing. I asked her to stop contact with my husband until we could figure out what was wrong between us, citing the more than twenty-year-commitment we had shared. She agreed, stating they were just friends, but she understood, as she had a commitment to her own husband to keep.

I believed them for a time, but later discovered he was calling her when we were on a family trip to Mexico. After I confronted him, he openly berated me for not being skilled at beach volleyball, and then made fun of me for drinking too much to dull the pain of his rejection. At the end of our vacation, however, he professed a change of heart and was profuse in his love for me. I recall feeling numb.

My senses were dulled, but I wasn't completely blind to his failures. Our business was shrinking, and I was upset that Paul was making financial decisions without consulting me. Yet I would bear the consequences with him. I obtained my nursing license and started working more than fifty hours a week as a nurse to keep our family financially afloat. My life had changed drastically. At times Paul was angry at the long hours I worked, saying I was putting my job above my family and our relationship. I became anxious and unsettled; he was rejecting and unkind.

One day, traveling home from a busy day of working on call, I was hit by an uninsured motorist on the driver's side, deploying my airbag. I walked away but my car was totaled. I called Paul to pick me up, I had refused an ambulance ride to the hospital. His first words were "Was it your fault?" with no apparent concern for me.

That car crash came to represent the reality of my marriage when I discovered Paul continued to have contact with the other woman. He was speeding along, paying no attention to his surroundings, and wrecking my life. I had tried to give him my best, and lost so much of myself, and he didn't even care enough about me to be loyal.

I confided in another couple and they helped me confront Paul. He admitted an emotional affair but denied any physical contact. I wasn't sure I believed him, but he agreed to cut it off and be accountable to our friends. But we had had been through this before with these same friends and their involvement hadn't made any difference in Paul's life. I doubted this time would end any differently and found myself losing all hope.

Without telling Paul, I sought counseling for myself. I shared with my counselor Joe how I wanted to be done with my marriage, but was surprised when he said I hadn't hit the wall yet. His question: "Was I ready to raise my kids alone?" made me realize I wasn't ready.

Joe coached me how I could stay married and not ride Paul's roller coaster. This was intriguing. I learned I could separate my heart from Paul by creating a bubble around it. I could let harsh criticism or anger hit this bubble and fall off. Surprisingly, it worked! Even though I was in a marriage that lacked mutuality, the bubble helped protect my heart so I didn't feel so much pain. I gained confidence by making some changes that I could control, and things actually seemed to improve in my marriage.

Paul began treating me as precious and honored. He hired a friend to clean our house, since I was working long hours. One night I came home to a beautiful bouquet of roses and a card. He did laundry and cooked dinner. I felt supported. He wrote in the card that the second half of our lives was going to be better than the first. The reassurance gave me hope to keep going, and I tried not to worry that this upswing might be followed by another dramatic drop. Instead, I continued to focus on how to change myself.

A few months later, I remember feeling deep uncertainty... aware in my gut that he was keeping secrets again, hiding something. I began to feel anxious and unsettled, sick to my stomach. Just as I was gathering the courage to question him, he came clean. He had been scheming to take me away on a cruise for our twenty-fifth wedding anniversary. He made all the arrangements, even calling my boss to request the time off work! He gave me a week's notice, just long enough to do a little shopping to prepare.

We had an idyllic time. The cruise was fun; my only small disappointment was that Paul didn't take the hint I was interested in having the captain renew our vows. We swam in turquoise blue waters, ate excellent food, and wandered new locations. After the ship docked in Miami, we checked into a hotel directly across from the beach. As we walked towards the surf, my eyes caught a familiar face. Pastor Scott and Jan, close friends from Seattle, were standing in the sand facing us. He had his Bible open and proceeded to lead us into a vow-renewal ceremony that Paul had thoughtfully planned as a surprise. Wow! That culmination of our anniversary trip completely settled for me any insecurities about our marriage. I was so happy, and relieved that we had weathered such a hard time but were now past it!

Once home, our construction business continued to shrink, and the threat of bankruptcy became real. I knew this was hitting Paul hard, as he took pride in being a good provider. His anger continued to rear its ugly head. I encouraged him, telling him "at least we have each other." I believed that the vow renewal was a firm line in the sand that settled our commitment. We'd successfully made it through twenty-five years and a lot of difficulty. What could possibly break that commitment now?

The answer to that question came when I was asked to speak at a women's retreat. It was the first opportunity for me to revisit my love of teaching since I went back to nursing. After the retreat, Laurel called me to her house and told me she had something hard to show me. She pulled up

*Paul's dating profile on her computer. I recall feeling devastated; it didn't seem possible. I was in agony.*

*I could only keep it from Paul for a few hours before calling him to tell him what I'd seen. He stayed calm. It appeared to be a mistake—something inadvertent or that someone else did. We talked it out, and after many tears on my part, I believed him. I had felt so secure, so this betrayal didn't fit what my gut was telling me. But a tiny question remained because I trusted Laurel. I worried that I would lose her friendship if she didn't believe him. Time would tell who I could really trust.*

*More surprises followed. At my nephew's wedding I discovered that Paul had bought a Jaguar. I was angry that he would spend money on something frivolous we couldn't afford, and embarrassed that his family knew but I didn't. He said he bought it for me as a surprise—that I had always wanted one, and it was for us to enjoy together. I didn't remember ever wanting a four-door Jag. But by the end of our conversation somehow, I was at fault and he gave me the silent treatment.*

*He put a lock on his cell phone and started keeping it in his car at night. In addition, there was money that couldn't be accounted for. I began acting like a detective, looking at his bank statements and emails. When I found something to question, he always provided an answer that seemed believable and I came away confused. Paul's responses made me feel crazy, overly suspicious, or to blame for the problems we were having. I didn't like myself when I stopped trusting. I couldn't trust my gut; it wasn't reliable.*

*The steep drop in our relationship continued when Paul took a position with a company in Idaho that supplied interior design services and products for high-end homes. His job involved socializing with clients and coworkers, and alcohol flowed freely. To discourage him going out without me, I started joining him.*

"When you continue to offer yourself in relationship to people who consistently mistreat you, disrespect you, control you, abuse you, and use you, you will feel sicker and sicker."[25]

*One night, we went together to a local bar with dancing. It was not a comfortable environment for me, which began to annoy him after he'd had a few drinks. He began to berate me verbally and called me a bitch. Instead of leaving, I started drinking more to fit in better. The night ended with him engaging me romantically. I felt close to him, even though I got there by ignoring the abusive words and becoming who I thought he wanted me to be. I regretted pursuing him at the expense of caring for my own heart.*

*I longed to be real, honest, and whole; the same person in all places, no matter what it cost me. I hated my insecurity, lack of confidence, and need for Paul's approval. I felt a constant, underlying sadness and wondered how I would ever get off his roller coaster ride.*

# 7

# Scapegoat

Cinderella **returned home** and hid the cherished glass slipper in her room. The next day, the duke began searching the entire kingdom for the girl whose foot fit the glass slipper left on the palace steps. When Cinderella heard the news, she got a dreamy look in her eyes. The prince was looking for her!

But the stepmother saw the dreamy look, became suspicious, and locked Cinderella in her room. **Isolating** Cinderella **prevented her from talking** to others about the abuse, which of course would tarnish the stepmother's reputation.

## 7.1 The Plan Not to Tell

Thanksgiving was fast approaching, and with it was an inherent expectation we spend time with my folks. This was out of the question. Neither Mike or I could fathom spending any time with my father given what we now knew. As it was, my mom had already caught me in a lie. She wanted to get together, so I told her Kenney had an event. But, when she responded by saying I had already gone to the event and told her about it, I knew I was busted.

Unsure how to proceed, Mike and I turned to Janis for advice. She agreed it was a good idea not to raise my parents' suspicions about what I was undergoing. She gave me the same warning Walter had given: To tell my parents what I was going through would only make my situation worse.

With Janis's help, I came up with a plan and called my mom to ask if we could meet for coffee. She sensed something was wrong, and I confessed I was dealing with some depression. "Can we talk about it tomorrow mom?" I asked. She agreed, and reminded me my aunt Penny, her sister, was visiting and would be joining us. I wondered if that was a God thing, maybe her presence would be helpful?

I was nervous. In the car on the way to Starbucks, I rehearsed what Janis and I planned for me to say. Right about then, I saw a vivid rainbow in the sky. It was most unusual because it hadn't been raining. In the years to come, many times when I prayed for my mom I would be reminded of that rainbow. It served as a promise from God that I would survive the overwhelming "flood" of sorrow I felt about the deterioration of our relationship.

I got to Starbucks and ordered. My mom and Penny came in shortly afterwards. Putting her hand on my shoulder my mom said, "I have been so worried about you. What's wrong?" I told her to get her coffee and we would talk. After they sat down, I said, "As I told you yesterday, I have been depressed and am working with a counselor. I wanted to let you know, I'm going to need some space and time to work through some things, so this year we won't be getting together with you and dad for the holidays."

My mom responded rather quickly, "Well, what's wrong?" I told her I wasn't ready to talk about it. She persisted. "I am your mother and want to know. I'm worried!" I continued with my rehearsed script, "I'm just working through some things that happened when I was a kid." Without much thought, she said, "Was it your dad?" I hadn't prepared for this and began to panic. I asked her what she meant. She went on to ask if my dad had done something. The tears started to flow, revealing the answer. And then she said, "Well I don't doubt it."

## 7.2 Change of Plans

Dumbfounded. That's all I can say. I mean if my daughter told me she was depressed and getting help for things that happened in her childhood, my first reaction would not be to suspect my husband of sexual abuse. That would actually be the furthest thing from my mind. Had she seen something? Had she suspected it?

I was thinking it, but my aunt Penny was the one to ask if she had ever suspected "this" was going on. She said no but went on to talk at length of my dad's other "sexual trysts." She started with the infidelity I already knew about. However, my dad's affair with Patsy, the lounge waitress, was much more involved than I realized. I heard details that broke my heart.

As my mom talked, waves of guilt washed over me. Now my crisis was overwhelming her. I tried to make her feel better, and said things like, "This is a generational curse, mom." AKA, it's not all his fault. "What do you mean?", she asked.

"You remember, dad told us several times recently that he was sexually molested growing up," I said. My mom looked at me like I was crazy. "You were sitting right there when he told us, mom." I said. She responded, "I don't remember that."

"A typical molester is one who was himself wounded early in life. Perhaps he was unwanted, neither valued as a person, nor nurtured by affectionate love from his parents. Perhaps he was abused sexually, beaten physically, emotionally abused, or neglected." [26]

I did. We had been in mixed company. The subject of child abuse came up, and my dad surprised all of us by blurting out, "Well, that happens to everyone." His words were shocking, and his tone alarming. Clearly, he was minimizing the trauma caused by abuse. My mom shot him a look of disbelief, and an awkward silence ensued. My dad then described an encounter he had as a child with an uncle in the back seat of a car. A year or two later, when again referencing this same incident, he went out of his way to emphasize the trivial impact it had on him.

The rest of the conversation with my mom that day is a blur. Our coffee date concluded with a discussion of how to best move forward. It was clear that neither Penny nor my mom had any clue what to do. My only idea was to get some advice from Janis. My mom agreed and left with Penny, intending to keep our conversation confidential.

## 7.3 Surprised by Selfishness

I was standing in the lobby of Janis's office the next day, when my mom arrived. I smiled at her, and as the two of us walked towards the elevators she said, "I can't leave him, Laurie." I didn't know what to say, so I responded, "I'm not asking you to."

"Telling the people in your family how you were hurt is the most expedient form of healing. Now you are finally free to speak the truth." [27]

We rode the elevators up to the third floor in silence. But my thoughts weren't quiet. I couldn't believe it! She wanted to stay with a man who taught a toddler to have oral sex? Seriously, is there nothing he could do that would be worthy of leaving him?

We got off the elevator and were ushered into Janis's office. After I explained what had happened in the coffee shop, Janis turned her attention to my mom. Much to my dismay, my mom did not express any concern for my well-being. Instead, she talked about my dad. On one hand, she didn't know if she could live with him and not say something about the alleged abuse. On the other hand, she really didn't want him to find out. Why? What reason did she have? I expected her to say, "He'll be angry, and I'm afraid of what he'll do to Laurel." But instead, she said, **"I am being treated like a queen for the first time in my life and I don't want it to stop."**

My initial response was one of shock and disbelief. I was in a crisis and she was worried about enjoying herself with the man who hurt me? It was unthinkable! I looked at Janis, embarrassed for my mom, then assumed the familiar role of caretaker. Instead of telling my mom how much her response hurt me, I offered to do whatever she wanted to make it better *for her*. Did she want me to go and tell him myself? I would. Did she want me to keep it a secret? I would support that as well.

---

"A great deal of variation exists in the aggressiveness of deniers in protecting the offender. Some are completely self-involved and ignorant of the ongoing abuse. Their response to disclosure of abuse shows a lack of compassion for their children and a selfish focus on their own lives." [28]

---

Ultimately, my mom decided to move forward without telling him anything. She would go home and encourage my dad to support my request for space and time to work through some problems in counseling.

We left the office, and I wasn't sure what hurt more: what my dad had done to me, seeing my mom's pain when I told her about it, or her current lack of concern for me. Could I have prevented all this by sticking to the plan? The burden was great.

I have thought a lot about it in the years that followed. Just as Janis and Walter had warned, my parents' awareness of my recovered memories complicated my healing process. But I have come to believe this is what God allowed to happen because it was best for me in the long run. In the years to come, it was actually my dad's behavior that convinced me (and maybe others) my memories were not false, but very, very true.

## 7.4 Acting Guilty

Mike and I were not surprised when later that week my mom called and said, "He knows." Apparently, when the shock wore off, she packed a bag, put it in the trunk of her car, and planned to leave my dad when he wasn't looking. Obviously, I wasn't the only one afraid of him. We both were.

Before she had the chance to escape, he discovered the packed bag and he forced her to explain. No surprise, he denied any wrongdoing, and then left the house for several hours. Later, he claimed he had gone to a nearby casino to "think." However, when my husband, the detective, later reviewed the casino security video footage from that night, as suspected, my dad was never there. Why lie? Mike maintained, "This is what guilty people do. When confronted, they run away to think and get their story straight."

Although we encouraged my mom to leave and stay with family, she chose otherwise. When my dad returned home later that evening, he cried, and was adamant he had never touched me. So, Mom stayed with him after all.

Meanwhile, Mike and I decided to contact my dad personally and sent the following email:

*Subject: Our Relationship*
*Dear Dad,*
*The abuse I experienced from you as a child has come back in*

*memories and emotions so I cannot talk or be around you at this time.*
*Please don't call or try to see me or my family.*
       *I love you, Laurel*

Reading this email today is rather difficult. Why I would write such a "nice" email that includes "Dear," "Please," and "love" given the circumstances? Why didn't I express anger, or tell him how hurt I was?

---

"When you break a family rule, you feel terrified contemplating it, wonderful while you are doing it, and guilt-ridden afterwards." [29]

---

Why? Because I had no backbone whatsoever and felt guilty. What did I have to feel guilty for? I felt responsible for what I was putting my family through. I also feared my dad's anger. I knew what he was capable of, and I believed it was not only possible but likely that he would get mad enough to come after me physically.

My dad responded to my email and agreed to stay away from my family and me, adding, "Well, if you said it happened then it must be true." The sarcasm revealed his anger, only serving to increase my already-heightened fear and anxiety.

## 7.5 Childlike Fear

The following day, Mike went to work, Kenney went to school, and I struggled to know what to do with myself. One thing was sure, I was not going to stay home alone. What if my dad came looking for me? When a dear friend Marci called and heard the fear in my voice, she invited me over. I went to her house and remained there the entire day. It felt like I was living a nightmare, that this was someone else's life and not my own.

The next day I dragged myself to work and immediately pulled our office manager aside. Sue was a confident, strong, and vivacious woman whose own family had also been touched by incest. Knowing she had brokenness like mine in her own family made entrusting her with my unfolding nightmare easier. I gave her a description of my dad and told her to tell him to leave if he ever showed up at the office. If he refused, I asked her to call 911.

It is not lost on me, that the fear that surfaced after the revelation of abuse was likely the same fear I had lived with my whole childhood. How many times did my dad threaten me not to tell? What did he say would happen if I did? Clearly, a part of me was still under his spell and believed every word of it.

## 7.6 Who's the Victim?

The next two months, I saw Janis one-to-two times a week. My work with her was aimed at how to cope with my new personal reality and what ended up being months of correspondence with my parents and other family members. My dad wanted to see me; I knew why. He wanted the chance to convince me of his innocence. It worked with my mom, and I'm sure he thought he could manipulate me as well.

It had only taken a few weeks for my mom to go from, "I don't doubt it," to, "I don't think he did it." She said this to me on the phone one day while I was at work. Why did she feel that way? She stated my dad was not responding like she expected him too. She and I both thought there would be a big blow up, like those we had seen in the past. Instead, my dad cried, there were tears, sorrow, and apparent confusion.

From my husband's and my vantage point, it was clear my dad had wisely chosen to play the role of the victim. In the coming months, he acted like the poor, falsely accused father who loved his daughter. And of course, if he was the victim, that meant I was the abuser.

## 7.7 A Far-Fetched Defense

On numerous occasions my dad violated our agreement to not contact me. The first time, it came in the form of a letter my mom and dad both signed. In it, they denied any wrongdoing, and cited it was not possible for my dad to have sexually abused me because he had never been alone with me my entire childhood!

Never alone with me? My mom worked full-time for most of my early childhood, and my dad was often charged with watching me. Nevertheless, how could any father say he was never alone with his child? Were there no doors in the entire house?

In the letter, my dad also stated how much he loved and adored me. As I read it, I couldn't help but wonder where this dad had been my whole life? It was the first time he had ever expressed any love for me, and I was in my early forties by now. I do remember, on one occasion, he called me, "honey." I was in the second grade, riding in the truck with him near our home and I found it so unusual I never forgot it. I didn't respond to the letter.

### 7.8 What about the Kids?

Eventually, my parents found out we had told both of our kids what was happening. My mom, speaking for both her and my dad, conveyed how shocked and dismayed they were. However, there had been no way to avoid it. First of all, one of them still lived at home. Kenney, a senior in high school, had approached me one evening and asked what was wrong. "What do you mean?" I asked. He said, "Mom, I'm not stupid. I can see you're upset; I know there's something going on." Choosing my words carefully, I gave him an overview of what I had learned about my past and how my parents were responding.

I'll never forget what happened next. With compassion in his eyes, and a calm assurance, Kenney looked across the kitchen counter and said, "Mom, I believe you and it wasn't your fault."

My eighteen-year-old son stated what I often wished others would have said. Years later, family would express how they wanted to help me during this time but didn't know what to do. I thought about it, and to be honest, there really wasn't much they could have done other than believe me and affirm my innocence.

My daughter was across the country finishing up the last two years of her degree at a private university. We told her as well, this disclosure coming after both Mike and I realized that if my dad had abused me, it was entirely possible he also abused my children.

The day this realization hit me was a rough one. The "what ifs" threw us into a crisis. I felt awful and blamed myself for putting them at risk. Mike talked to both kids and reassured them if something happened, we needed to know. Both denied any sexual experiences with my dad, but this really didn't put us at ease. After all, if I had repressed the trauma of my past, so could they.

We took this concern to Janis on a subsequent appointment. What she shared allowed us to calm down and refocus on God. She said, "If something happened to one or both of them, then one day they will have the same opportunity for healing that you now have." I hold that truth close to my heart and to this day it continues to give me peace.

## 7.9 Losing My Mom

After several months, my phone conversations with my mom became more strained, and fewer. I could see the writing on the wall and a new fear overtook me, that of losing my mom. In the past, whenever my dad was mad at me, he withdrew from relationship. As a child, this often equated to days of the silent treatment. As an adult, whenever I was "in trouble," a sudden change in my mom's correspondence would often be the first clue there was a problem.

I don't know why I expected her to behave any differently than she had before, but I did. I was there for her all those years, listening, encouraging, and giving suggestions on her adult problems with my dad. Now that I needed her, surely, she would do the same for me, right? Wrong. She pulled back.

---

"The pain of confronting your family is equal to the strength you will gain from doing it." [30]

---

I know my mother never intended to hurt me. She was a victim too. My dad held her as his emotional hostage and betrayed her many times during their marriage. Nonetheless, she played a key role in my ongoing abuse. With the exception of the first few weeks, my mom conspired with my dad to cover up the truth of what he had done. This would be the most painful part of my recovery. I considered it a betrayal, one that I never thought her capable of.

My communication with my mom at this time was very infrequent, despite an initial plan to talk each Monday. She was supposed to call when my dad left the house for a standing commitment. Every Monday I looked for that call, but most of the time it never came.

## 7.10 Feeling Guilty

My dad continued to contact me, despite the commitment he made not to. He called and emailed, and each time I responded by falling apart emotionally. In February, Mike intervened and sent an email to my dad asking for any further contact with me to go through him. I agreed this was necessary but worried my mom would stop corresponding as well. I sent her a card, expressing my continued love for her, and near the end of February, I received an invitation for lunch to celebrate my upcoming birthday.

The invitation really gave me an emotional boost. I had renewed hope we could have a relationship despite the boundaries I had with my dad. The morning of our lunch date, I spent some time with God in prayer. An image of my mom kneading some dough came to mind. I wondered if she was going to try to "work some things out" over lunch.

My time with God that morning prior to lunch with my mom was well spent and prepared me for our conversation. However, the optimism and hope I arrived with quickly turned to pain when my mom seemed determined to discuss my dad while we waited to order. She said, "Your dad is so upset and wants to see you. Don't you miss him?" "No mom, I don't!" I responded.

I repeated the purpose of the boundary; I needed time and space to heal. In response, she questioned my symptoms. "I wonder if you are going through menopause?" As if hormones were responsible for my PTSD. A lump in my throat formed, and my eyes welled up. "Don't cry," my mom said. How many times had I heard that growing up? It was never okay to show genuine emotion.

She continued to talk about my dad and support his innocence. And when it became obvious I wasn't going to budge, she told me my dad was going to have a polygraph. I got very upset. "Mom, you have been saying for months he's going to get a polygraph. What's the holdup?"

My response caught her off guard, and she seemed surprised that so much time had passed. And then, because of something Janis had warned me about, I discouraged the idea. I made it clear that if my dad did have a polygraph, Mike and I would need to be involved. Who performed the test and other details would be important to agree upon upfront.

As we finished our meal, I drummed up the courage to confront my mom about her lack of communication with me. When I asked why she wasn't keeping our commitment to talk on Mondays, she apologized stating, "I just cannot face this." Even though I had said many times I didn't want to talk about my dad, it was becoming clear that merely talking to me was hard for her. She was sticking by his side, and slowly letting go of me.

We ended our lunch, and as I walked away, her last words to me were, "Don't forget I love you." It felt like a final goodbye. I was so overwhelmed. She was very important to me, and even if she wasn't going to play the role of my mom in this crisis, I still felt strongly about having her in my life. Almost as soon as I got in the car, I felt guilty. Guilty for pressuring her to call me, guilty for getting upset about the polygraph.

The next morning, while praying, the verse "Jesus wept" came to mind.[31] The shortest verse in the Bible is one of the most powerful testimonies of our God's compassion. I would be reminded of God's sorrow over my loss many times in the following years. He was with me, just as he had always been, grieving over the devastation sin was having on my life and family.

## 7.11 Scapegoating

My brother always called on my birthday. He lived in Seattle, and was married with two young children, but was good at staying in touch. Actually, he was better at it than I was. So, it was very unusual when I didn't hear from him. I let several weeks go by, and then called him, suspecting my parents had violated our agreement and talked to him about my claims of sexual abuse. Sure enough, I was right.

The phone call was very painful; Brett was angry. Very angry. He talked about my parents' pain over both the allegations and subsequent deterioration of our relationship. I did my best to explain to my brother what had led to the discovery of abuse, but he didn't believe my dad capable of what I described. He questioned my choice of counselors, questioned if I had misplaced my trust, and believed I had "ideas" planted in my mind.

I invited him to come to counseling with me, so he could meet my counselor and find out more about what I was going through, and he declined. Before I hung up, I cautioned him about allowing my dad to be alone with his children. He thought this was ridiculous and was angered even more by the concern. However, I had been worrying about the safety of his children for quite some time and wasn't sorry I brought it up. Needless to say, the call ended poorly.

Instead of my parents keeping our problems between us, they told their side of the story proactively to align my brother against me. They went out of their way to destroy my credibility. In the years that followed, Brett heard them say many things about their ongoing problems with me. Then Brett, when talking to me, would repeat what they told him. Most of the time, what I heard my parents were saying was not true. But, when I defended myself, Brett didn't know who to believe and told me so.

---

"Scapegoat: a person or group made to bear the blame for others or to suffer in their place." [32]

"Scapegoating enables the family members who point the finger to operate under the illusion that all is well with them, and that any family problems originate with the person targeted for scapegoating." [33]

Eventually, I made it a personal goal not to triangulate by discussing my parents with Brett. He was enjoying a relationship with my dad, and it was never my intent to interfere with that. However, most of the time this decision meant the only information he got was from my parents.

## 7.12 Navigating Birthdays and Holidays

In the past, when birthdays were celebrated, they triggered communication and relationship. But now everything had changed. Birthdays and holidays trigged awkward and painful interactions. None of us knew how to act given the new "normal."

My mom and I saw each other one more time that spring. We met for coffee to celebrate her birthday. This time, she didn't pressure me to see my dad. She brought up my recovery and asked if I was doing any better, and then said, "I just can't face it." This wasn't new, but what she said next was. "If it's true, what does that say about me?" Her reflection made me sad, and I tried to encourage her, saying "It doesn't say anything about you."

It was a short visit, but I cherished every minute. Later, on the phone, she told me that when she got home that day my dad was very angry. "He was sure we had spent the whole time talking about him; he went on about it for hours," she said. Obviously, it was costly for her to see me and have a relationship me.

I was once again struck with how my recovery was affecting my mom's life and causing her so much pain. Eventually I was able to put the guilt where it belonged, on my dad. But first, I had to undo years of conditioning. Unfortunately at the time, being the scapegoat felt right and normal.

My Dad's birthday rolled around. It had always been hard to pick out a card for him. Nothing seemed to fit, and this year was worse than ever.

Someone could make a killing if they came up with a line of cards for strained relationships. I can't be the only one feeling this challenge! Somehow, I managed to find one, and sent if off in an attempt "to do the right thing."

Not long after, in a rare phone call, my mom told me my card had upset my dad. She said he was "beside himself" because he didn't know what it meant. At the same time, my mom talked of her own deepening depression saying, "I see abuse on TV and am worried about what people will think."

As Mother's Day approached, I was given the opportunity to give the Sunday message at church. At first, the idea seemed like pouring salt on an already gaping wound. However, that notion was turned on its head when I read a book that encouraged writing a tribute to your parents. Exodus 20:12 says, "Honor your father and mother so that you may live long in the land the Lord your God is giving you."

The author of the book had done this for his own mother, and although he had a good relationship with her, he challenged readers by saying even if you have been abused or disappointed by a parent, you can find something to commend.

I delivered the Mother's Day message and in it read a tribute that I wrote about my own mother. I then made a copy of the tribute and included it in a Mother's Day card I mailed to her. Despite how I felt at the time, I made the choice to honor her in this way. I knew it pleased God, and to be honest, it was good for me to remember all the many ways my mom had come through for me during my life. It helped balance my disappointment about her betrayal with the things she had done right. There is nothing included in this tribute that isn't 100% true, and I have never regretted taking the time, as painful as it was then, to formulate it.

## THE WORLD'S FINEST MOTHER

*I guess I'm like many others; I have an awesome mother. Here are some of the reasons why I believe Beverly Smith, is one of the world's finest:*

**Words.** *She swore only one time in my whole childhood. It was at my brother in a Woolworth Store in Seattle. He was five years old, and* *as I recall he had it coming!*

*Support. My mom attended sports events I played in, awards ceremonies, parent teacher conferences, and pretty much any other thing she could, to show me her support. I always felt like I was a priority for her.*

*Beautiful. In her younger years, her beauty was often noted in big ways. She was voted homecoming queen, cherry blossom queen, and I am sure got other awards I don't even know about. But her beauty never faded. When I was a teen, people often confused her for my sister! My mom is gorgeous.*

*Thoughtful. My mom remembers the small things that others may not. Even when I was a teen, she would leave me an Easter basket with a small gift and candy. She sends me home with little gifts every time I visit. She is very thoughtful, but at the same time funny because this same gesture done by her mom for years made her crazy! She agonizes over what gift to get people for Christmas, to the point it makes her almost sick.*

*Show stopper. For some reason, one of the most vivid memories I have as a child with my mom is the time her foot got stuck in the escalator at the old Crescent Dept store. It threw everyone into a panic. They ended up turning off the power so that they could get her free. She literally had everyone stopped in their tracks!*

*Rose. I think my mom's favorite flower describes her best, the rose. Yes, a rose sums up her perfectly. She is classy, fragile during the winter seasons, but oh so hardy, always bouncing back when the weather changes. And beautiful? My mom is breathtaking and her blossoms unforgettably fragrant. I love you mom.*

## 7.13 Fought For

My dad continued to disregard the boundary of no communication and kept asking for a meeting with me. On one hand, I didn't want to see the man. On the other, I didn't want to hide; I wanted to stand up for myself. But Mike and Janis were emphatic; I wasn't ready. I needed to be stronger before I faced him. After some discussion, it was decided that Mike would call my dad.

---

"The kind of punishment families mete out when you break the no-talk rule about abuse fall on a continuum:
- Healthier families will react with shock and sadness to hear of your suffering.
- Less healthy families are disbelieving, labeling you as crazy or living in a fantasy world.
- Families in total denial will ostracize or disinherit the survivor.
- Extremely pathological families threaten violence or death." [34]

---

In their brief exchange, my dad rambled on about his innocence. "I am never going to admit to this," he said. He again pleaded with Mike to let me sit down and talk to him. When Mike said, "No," he responded, "Maybe we should terminate the relationship. This is draining me." It was all about him.

The conversation ended with the two of them agreeing to meet. If my dad couldn't meet with me, I guess Mike was the next best thing. All I could think was, he must be desperate. He had never liked Mike.

The meeting was held at a truck stop restaurant near my parent's home. Mike brought a coworker with him, who sat in a nearby booth unbeknownst to my dad. His presence provided Mike assurance that should emotions escalate, someone would be there to prevent things from getting out of hand.

### Mike's Description of the Meeting with Laurel's Dad

*We met at the truck stop by their house. A co-worker followed me because he didn't trust me. The meeting started with Larry saying he has always liked and respected me. I pointed out that was nonsense and that we merely tolerated each other.*

*Larry was all about Larry. He complained that this was going to be his legacy and how he would always be remembered. Larry pointed out how Laurel had sent him this awful email written in red that was full of hate. At this time since I couldn't punch him in the face, I decided to have some fun other ways and began pushing his buttons to the point he got up and almost left.*

*He said that Laurel was telling everyone about this and it was ruining him. I pointed out that was not true, that she had not said a word to anyone. He was the one doing all the talking. He was the one that told Brett, not her.*

*He said Laurel told Kelsey and Kenney. I told him that I did that, which he said was poor parenting and I said he shouldn't talk about parenting skills. Since it was getting heated, he went back to the woe-is-me story.*

*He said that he thought the counselor was putting things in Laurel's head. I said I didn't think so and suggested we all go to see the counselor. He said no, that counseling was for people who were crazy, and he wasn't crazy. I did suggest that he might look into what she was going through just so he would understand better.*

*Larry said he was never going to take a polygraph because Laurel would never accept it. Of course, nobody asked her, he just assumed. Also, he said that he talked to his attorney about this and was advised not to take the polygraph test. Now I am a bit suspicious, but after being a police officer for twenty-five years it is hard not to be. I also will note that I have never talked to someone who has not done anything wrong that needed to talk to a lawyer, but that's just me. I asked why he needed an attorney and he said that I was trying to turn the whole thing around on him.*

*He made all kinds of excuses:*

- *"I could not have done it. I am not circumcised, and it takes a lot to excite me." Ok, what does that have to do with anything?*
- *"Men are not excited by little girls." This one also took me by surprise, and I had to point out the billion-dollar porn*

*industry says differently. I was then told I had an answer to everything.*

- *I was pushing him a lot and he got so mad he said, "Why would I pick Laurel when I had a daughter with Downs Syndrome that would have enjoyed it?"*

*I didn't then and still don't think he meant to say that, it was just that I had him so pissed off. I actually thought he might pop a blood vessel and die right there. Either way, he left mad and I had a great witness that I didn't touch him. Laurel's mom called later and said she had hoped for a better outcome.*

Mike stood up for me in ways I had never experienced before. I felt protected, fought for, and loved. One of the good things that resulted from this horrific time in my life was a deeper relationship with my husband. I was in awe of him. He was heroic and I'm grateful he was willing to take this journey with me. I was told by my counselor that not all spouses will.

After Mike and my dad's meeting I received this email from my mom.

**Sent:** *Monday,* **May 18, 2009** *9:35 a.m.*
**To:** *Laurel*
**Subject:** *Thank you for your correspondence*

*Laurel, I don't know how to express myself especially after the lovely card, note, and enclosure. The events between all of us seem unbelievably tragic and hard to swallow. It humbles me that your sermon expressed so many traits that I wish I could feel were deserved and left out the failures that seem overwhelming to me as your mom. Please keep upper most in your mind that you will always be a special part of me and loved deeply. It seemed that the conclusion of Larry and Mike's visit didn't accomplish the goal (being able to meet and discuss personally), but if it helps you to heal and move on that's the important thing. It might help us as well, but I'm not opposed to our "meetings" if you so choose. I meant to tell you how radiant you looked when we had coffee last time; by the way you most certainly didn't hurt my feelings*

*in any way!*
*Love, Mom*

## 7.14 Angry

After six months of dealing with my dad's denial, lies, and betrayals, my feelings of shame and guilt were gradually giving way to anger. More and more, I found myself wanting to tell my dad off. He had robbed me of so much and I couldn't do a thing about it.

---

"If your family could respond the way you wanted, you would not have had to repress the memory in the first place. As you handle their denials, you are given an opportunity to see the family dysfunction more clearly. You do not have to convert them; you only have to free yourself." [35]

---

And then, for the first time, I found myself getting angry at my mom too. I started to see the part she played in ruining my reputation with other family members. On a regular phone call, my grandma (my mom's mom) surprised me by saying, "Shame on you." When I asked what she was talking about she said, "You know the right thing to do." Still confused, I asked what she was referring to and was told, "I never thought you would do something like this." "Like what, Grandma?" To which she replied, "How could you not invite your parents to your own son's graduation?"

I didn't feel I had a choice to keep silent, so I told her. "Mom is invited, but not my dad. I haven't seen him for months because I am having memories of being sexually molested by him growing up." The conversation ended shortly after and I was again devastated. Mike called my grandma the next day to explain, and was told, "Larry says he didn't do it." She had called my folks after talking to me.

My mom didn't try to cover for me with my grandma when the subject of Kenney's graduation came up. Instead, she made me look like the bad guy to protect her own image. In my next appointment with Janis, I expressed that "My mom is making me the abuser."

In my anger, I wrote my mom and told her how hurt I was, and not to contact me anymore. I regret this now. For one, I didn't talk to her personally about what happened with my grandma. I wished I had given her a chance to explain and talk about it. Secondly, I feel it was not right to address the conflict in an email.

The losses were starting to pile up and overwhelm me. I felt it was a very real possibility I would lose not only my mom, but my brother, and grandmother too.

## 7.15 Insight Through Friendship

My feelings about my mom remained very complex. Some days I was angry, others I missed her terribly and had great compassion for her. Much of this sympathy was born out of my relationship with Lynn.

It was unbelievable timing, but Lynn was doing what I had always wanted my mom to do. She was getting healthy, seeing a counselor, and making changes in her relationship with her husband. But, not without a cost. Paul responded with increased cruelty, unfaithfulness, and emotional volatility. I saw so much of my dad in him.

But as I witnessed how difficult it was for her to make progress, I realized some things. Lynn had a relationship with God, she had a close-knit group of friends, and a church community all of which served to hold her up during this volatile time of change with Paul. My mom had none of those things. Outside of her mom and sisters who lived across the state, she had no deep friendships, no church membership, and a lot of doubts about God.

Lynn was also aware of the uncanny similarities. Sometimes when I processed events and feelings about my mom with her, she was able to give me insight born out of experience. Looking at my mom's situation through the eyes of a beloved friend was a gift that kept me from getting bitter.

## 7.16 Escalating Pressure

The pressure to meet with my parents increased as extended family members became aware of the conflict and wanted us to reconcile. I heard different things from different people. Some said my dad claimed I was unwilling to meet with him and he didn't know why, or what was wrong. That was partially correct. I didn't want to meet with him.

Still others said my parents were reading books on False Memory Syndrome and felt sure I suffered from this. So, he did know what was wrong, but was playing the victim. His confused daughter was falsely accusing him because she was being manipulated by a counselor who put ideas in her head.

---

"Family members should:
- Validate the victim's feelings, "Thank you for sharing, I can't even imagine the pain you must feel."
- Refuse to take sides or mediate.
- Learn and get more information." Dr. Mary Dietzen

---

I was tired, tired of the conflict and tired of holding the boundary. I felt a lot of pressure and periodically reverted to feeling responsible for the family drama. When my brother and other family members asked me to give in and see my dad, I relented. I emailed my folks that I would agree to meet with them and a mediator.

I received this email back from my dad:

*Laurel,*

*We received your email and read it yesterday. We now have an understanding of repressive memory; we're aware that among respected psychiatrists there are both skeptics as well as believers. Laurel, I have lived in this body seventy-two years and I can tell you every bad thing I have ever done. This abusive act or any other act of molestation you think I might have done or would do is just not so.*

*Your present condition is upsetting and the fact that you have not improved lately bothers us. This has been hard here also; we are concerned and talk about it daily.*

*The prospect of a meeting with a mediator would be fine. But as I told Mike, I was willing to meet before at any time with you and a mediator. So, one has to wonder though: What is the purpose of the meeting now? What can be accomplished? What has changed that will help this be resolved.? Unless there is common ground to seek a resolution, I think it would put both of us through unwanted stress. If, however, a meeting could be structured to help get you out of the depression that would be worthwhile. Maybe you could send me a list of items you wish to talk about by email and get my response.*

*I'm sorry you feel we have said bad things about you to others, but until I know the specifics it's hard to address them. As you can see my writing is bad. But understand, you are in my thoughts daily and I would do anything in my power to help you heal.*

*Love dad*

It was hard to breathe. The letter, from my point of view, oozed with manipulation and was not in any way genuine or believable. After months of asking for a meeting, he flips the script and acts like the meeting was all my idea? I felt despondent. I was sinking now into a hole so deep I couldn't imagine getting out.

## 7.17 Polygraph

The one-year anniversary of my first recollection of sexual abuse was fast approaching and it had been three months since I had any contact with my parents. I went to the mailbox and discovered a statement from an attorney's office. In the envelope, there was also a letter from my dad.

*Mike, I hope this finds everyone well. I thought you and Laurel should know that I passed the polygraph test recently. Bev and I are*

*open to arranging a meeting with both of you and a mutually agreed upon mediator for the purpose of reconciling our relationship. We are available whenever it's convenient. Let us know.*
　　*Larry*

Confusion washed over me. Then horror. Were my worst fears coming true? Had I been wrong and put my family through this needless trial?

Mike was there, thank God, when I opened the mail. His response was much different than mine. Mike's nearly twenty-five years of experience as a detective led him to investigate the polygraph before placing his trust in it. The next day, he went to work and asked various experts in the field about the polygrapher and the statement that was sent to me.

Mike was told repeatedly, "You get what you pay for." My dad's lawyer had a reputation with the police department for doing questionable work in order to produce favorable outcomes for defendants. This particular polygrapher uses two graphs instead of the industry standard of three. Mike was also told that the two questions asked of my dad during the test were improperly worded. (The questions were included in the statement mailed to me.)

Mike was encouraged to get the actual tapes so others in the field could confirm the results. He contacted the attorney's office multiple times and was repeatedly denied access to the tapes. He was told my dad wouldn't release them. Why? Why deny access if you are innocent? Why had my dad sidestepped us when he knew we would want to be involved in the selection of who did the polygraph as well as the questions? And why did it take him one year before he took the test?

Later, I learned the answer to one of these questions. One weekend, my parents spent the night at my brother's house. During the visit, my brother found him and my nephew in the bathroom with the door shut. Brett told my dad this made him uncomfortable, and asked he not do so again. My dad, offended by the obvious lack of trust, immediately packed up and left with my mom. The next day, he took the polygraph. Dad had taken the polygraph not for me, but to salvage the relationship with my brother.

## 7.18 Protected

Although Mike and I didn't find the polygraph credible due to the lack of transparency surrounding it, it was brought to my attention that some of my family members felt differently. Eager to see a resolution to the crisis, we were encouraged to meet with my parents and a mediator to begin the process of reconciliation. Mike was adamantly opposed to the idea, I on the other hand was tired of the ongoing pressure and conflict and wanted to give in.

However, we received an email from my dad which stipulated that any meetings with a mediator could include no discussion of the past. That was a deal breaker. Janis, Mike and Walter all advised against it. Mike came up with an idea to contact my family. "I'll tell them it was my decision not to meet," he said. In this way, he hoped the blame would be directed at him, not me.

Mike then sent an email to my parents:

*Larry,*

*I read your last email with interest. I thought it a bit odd, so I have included it: "My belief that this meeting (with a mediator) is that we are searching for a way to proceed with our relationship, and any accusations about the past on either side will not be a part of the discussion. I would be interested what you think about this?"*

*What do I think? I think this is one of the oddest things I have ever read. If it wasn't for the past, there wouldn't be a problem. How would anyone ever think about moving forward without addressing the issue to begin with?*

*I must be going soft in the head to ever think this would work out. I have a large number of issues with some of the things that have gone on during the last year. Laurel has expressed to me a deep desire to let this all go and move on but isn't sure about a relationship right now. Her counselor has expressed some reservations about the whole idea of a meeting even with a third party. So, we come to the next roadblock. That is going to be me.*

*There is no way I am going to subject my wife, whom I love more than life itself, to what amounts to a three-ring circus. I look back at the last year and what she has been put through and have decided to put an end to it now. I think the best thing to do is what you said in our meeting. I think we should terminate the relationship because I don't see this ever going anywhere. I'm sorry but there is no way that I am putting Laurel through any more than she already has been.*

*I will be sending copies of this to Brett and uncle Rob not because I think or feel they have done anything wrong, but I want no mistake made in who wrote this or sent it.*

*Mike*

## 7.19 Cutting Ties

It is no surprise, that several in my family verbalized a strong reaction in defense of my dad in response to Mike's email. My actions were called hypocritical, my counselors discredited, and my recollections acknowledged but not completely embraced. It's also rather obvious that no one involved in these conversations seemed to comprehend the emotional trauma I was still experiencing, nor how it would be magnified when facing the man I believed was responsible.

Some simply wanted it to not be true, and the polygraph seemed to satisfy this desire, despite the information Mike gave them about it. If they didn't believe he could fabricate a polygraph, how could they believe he could molest a child? I can only imagine how relieved my dad was that his cover-up was working.

This was a low point for me. I felt I couldn't take it anymore; there seemed no answer to this dilemma. At the same time, I thought I could not survive the loss of my family. Janis encouraged me to let Jesus be the target. He could take the darts, I couldn't. In prayer I heard, "Encouragement will come; stand firm in the truth I have shown you."

I drafted and then sent a letter to my parents; I felt it was important if we were terminating the relationship for them to hear from me personally.

*Dear Mom and Dad,*

*I am writing this letter to you with my heart full of both love and sorrow. Although I appreciate your willingness to meet with me, after much prayer and consultation, I am going to decline the offer at this time. This was not an easy decision. Everything in me wants to do what I can to bring you comfort and reassurance that our relationship can be salvaged. Yet, it appears that we value different things and that a meeting may only make things worse...*

*As I have prayed about this decision, God dropped a passage in my heart. It is from Amos 3:3. It says, "How can two walk together unless they agree on the direction?"*

*I hope you understand my decision.*

*Laurel*

I learned later, that separation from my family was the most important task I needed to accomplish to get better. I needed to cut ties in order to focus on my own healing.

## 7.20 Hope for a Restored Soul

Around that time, a lightning bolt hit a tree in the front yard and it fell on the house. I came home one evening, saw the tree resting on the roof, blocking the front door, and wondered how things could get any messier in my life. Water damaged the flooring, branches pierced through the ceiling of several rooms in the house, and windows were shattered.

But the restoration of our home, although inconvenient, ended up being a blessing. The week prior to the accident, I told God in prayer that the old smelly house had turned out to be a lovely home. We had taken out walls, gotten new flooring and cabinets, and replaced the masonry. Sure, there were a few things, like the kitchen floor and the living room ceiling, that I would have loved to update; but overall, I was very happy there.

Can you believe that those few lingering improvements were the very things damaged in the storm? We got a new roof, a cathedral ceiling, a new tile floor in the kitchen, among other improvements. Insurance made $70,000 worth of repairs to our home for a $500 deductible fee.

God spoke to me through these circumstances. I believed that the storm in my life, that had done so much damage to my soul and family relationships, would one day be something I thanked God for. It would be the avenue through which He would give me the desires of my heart. My pain had a purpose.

This seemed to be confirmed, when one day, a friend described to me what she felt God impressed on her in prayer. God showed her that the tearing down of the "Old House" was completed, and now he was going to begin "The Rebuilding."

# Jillian

## Behind Closed Doors—A Buried Trauma Exposed

*I was very angry at how Laurel's family was treating her. I saw the effects of her dad's denial and her mom's support of him wear on her. There were days I wanted to just show up at his door and beat him up. Laurel and I spent many mornings on the phone encouraging each other and praying for each other.*

*Meanwhile, my struggles with Jacob continued to frustrate me. Although I wanted to believe we had made progress on our intimacy problems, there really was none. The truth was that I had finally accepted it as it stood. I heard him regularly say, "You just don't get a great sex life when you're older." I began to resign myself to mediocracy in the bedroom, believing that's all we would ever have.*

*But I wasn't ready to let go of the remodel project that was still unfinished. I tried and tried to get Jacob to move forward on what I wanted him to accomplish to no avail. I was sure my unhappiness was due to these external circumstances. One morning, Laurel asked me what Jacob did, that I could be thankful for. After some thought, one thing did come to mind. He was willing to vacuum the house. I hated vacuuming. I couldn't stand the noise as the vacuum started up. It was a chore I had delegated to my kids while they were home.*

*One Sunday at church, the pastor announced an upcoming Marriage Life Conference. They encouraged couples to attend. I went thinking the conference would fix him and help him see my side of things. I just knew it would make him become a better husband. What I didn't realize was how God would use it to heal me of a traumatic event from my past. A wound so painful I hadn't been able to face it for twenty-four years.*

*It happened without warning. The wives and husbands were in separate sessions. The speaker was talking about intimacy and how God uses our relationship with our husbands to help us grow closer to them and to God. She started talking about roadblocks that can rob us of fully experiencing God's best in our marriage relationships. "Some of you have had an abortion years ago. It was a painful time in your life." She went on to say that sexual sin can affect your intimacy with your husband. I felt like I was the only one in the room and she was talking directly to me.*

*At the end of that session the speaker prayed and asked God to show us if we needed God's healing and forgiveness from our past. As she prayed, I saw a picture in my mind. It looked like me, laying on an exam table in a hospital gown with feet up in stirrups. I was attached to a what looked like a vacuum hose. Fear gripped me. I felt dizzy. Was that really me? I wanted to convince myself it was someone else. I wanted to run and hide. My heart was pounding out of my chest. I could hardly breathe. I felt like running but could barely move. I felt exposed. I stuffed my feelings, trying to ignore them and the picture of the room in my mind.*

*That night as Jacob and I were lying in bed and talked about the conference, I told him the speaker talked about sexual sin and how that can affect our marriage relationship. I left out the part about what I had seen as she prayed. Jacob prayed his usual short prayer thanking God for me and asking Him to bless our marriage. I fell asleep but woke up in the middle of the night to the sound of a vacuum cleaner. I thought it was the maid outside our hotel room door. I listened, but nothing was there. I closed my eyes and the picture of me lying on the table accompanied the vacuum sound came to mind. My chest tightened. It was hard to breathe, and I started to panic. Instead of waking him up, I moved closer to my sleeping husband for comfort. I decided it was best to push it down and not invite his support.*

*For several nights, I couldn't sleep or get that picture out of my thoughts. Tears would roll down my face, as more pieces of my past would drift in. The memories always started with me in that exam room. Then I saw a woman coming in the room to check on me. She gave me some pills to take and left me alone in pain. I also remembered being at a cashier window handing over cash and signing a paper. Standing at that window, I heard words "double gestation." Horrified, I started to realize what all of it might mean.*

*As the reality that I might have had an abortion started to sink in, I wanted to kill myself. Doing myself in would be easier than admitting something that terrible. Shaking, I asked God to show me the truth. He gave me an idea. I looked up the number of my ex-husband and called it. He confirmed my suspicions. I sobbed as he told me it was true. We had aborted our twin babies. He wasn't ready to be a father. We had enough stress, as he put it, and it would be easier to start our relationship without the burden of another kid. I already had two. He had made the arrangements and I went along with it. He said he was sorry and had struggled with wanting to kill himself whenever he thought about it. I was angry at him and even more angry at myself. Why did I ever go along with it?*

*I hated myself for what I had done. I had been willing to do whatever it took to be loved. But despite the abortion and the efforts to save our relationship, our marriage had ended in divorce. I had not succeeded in saving anything, only causing death and destruction. Then I had buried the memory, too ashamed to face what I had done.*

*God had brought my dark secret to the light. What was I supposed to do now? Laurel had modeled what facing a painful past looked like. She was getting the help she needed. I wanted to do the same and get free from the overwhelming shame. But I was afraid to tell anyone, let alone Jacob. When we were dating, he had wrestled with the fact that I was divorced twice. He said he used to look down on people who were divorced until he met me.*

*He told me he decided it wasn't as bad as having an abortion. I agreed with him not realizing that later I would discover I was that woman. I was not only divorced twice but also had an abortion. What was he going to think of me now? I feared losing yet another relationship.*

*When I finally managed to tell him, his response was surprising. He held me and said we'd get through this. It was the first time in our marriage he had showed empathy for me. I knew I had to tell someone besides him or I would just bury it again. It had to stay exposed. I called Laurel and asked her to meet me for coffee. When it came time to leave for our meeting, fear rose up. Tapes were playing in my mind of shame and not being good enough. I wanted to cancel but didn't. It was a tearful confession. She was supportive and encouraged me to get help. She knew a friend, Grace, who also had an abortion. Through the help of Life Services, she had found healing. Not only that, she was now speaking about it and encouraging other women to get help and healing they needed. I was shocked that anyone could talk about this publicly. I could barely tell my husband and best friend.*

*Laurel said that I should call Grace and hear her story. It took me another two weeks to get up the courage to call her. She spoke freely about her abortion, not bound by fear and shame. She gave me the anonymous number to call and sign up for an abortion recovery group. Again, I was afraid to take that step. It would require me to be honest and open about one of my biggest failures.*

*I was on my usual mission to push forward and not look back. Instead of making the call to sign up for the class, I checked out the website and saw Life Services was having a volunteer training night. I decided I would just "help" other people who were facing unwanted pregnancies. I had already confessed it. Wasn't that enough? I signed up to volunteer.*

*However, God didn't let me off the hook so easily. When I attended orientation, they said if we had experienced an abortion, we would need to go through the abortion recovery class before volunteering. The leader asked by a show of hands how many of us had an abortion. Five out of nine women raised their hands. I found myself slowly raising my hand. There* went my plan to be anonymous. They had a signup sheet for the recovery class that Grace had suggested. I fought the temptation to leave. Waiting until most everyone had left, I walked over and signed up for healing._

In God's loving timing, He brought my abortion wound to the surface so I could be healed. The class was twelve weeks of hard work. At the end, we shared our stories with each other. There were tears shed and hearts healed. We had found forgiveness for ourselves. God set me free from the shame and pain I had buried for so many years. In time, like Grace, I too shared my abortion story and God's healing in public.

# Lynn

## Behind Closed Doors—Numb to the Danger

The desire for my own personal healing eventually equaled, and maybe exceeded, the desire to keep my marriage together. Still committed to Paul, I began to invest in things that made me happy and healthy apart from him. Things like counseling, reading books on how to live in an unhappy marriage, all moved me forward in my growth. Waiting on God, not Paul, became a goal of mine. I attempted to keep hope alive without holding my heart back while I waited.

Paul continued his roller coaster of feelings towards me, but I didn't ride it with him as often. The practices of speaking up and keeping a bubble around my heart were changing me, even though they didn't impact his behavior. I still felt distance between us and didn't trust him completely, but I began to be more authentic and less desperate. One night I had a dream that he was flying away forever. He had a business trip to the Ukraine planned, but I felt the dream was symbolic. I asked him to have lunch with me and spoke honestly. I explained that I felt his distance and didn't understand it. I wanted him to know he had a choice and didn't have to "fly away." Paul seemed impressed by my insight. I felt strong and free for speaking honestly. Later that dream would prove prophetic.

A word picture shared by Leslie Vernick in her book, _The Emotionally Destructive Relationship_, describes a healthy progression of responses to repeated harm. If the person you are sitting next to begins to kick you in the shin, you calmly speak up and tell them to stop. If that doesn't work, you move back out of their easy reach, and if they still persist, you stand up and yell at them to knock it off! I had improved at speaking up and pulling back (the bubble) but standing up would require a much steeper learning curve.[36]

One afternoon I arrived a few minutes early to my next patient appointment and decided to call Paul. There was a pause when we connected, and then I heard his voice clearly, but as if in the background: "I just want to be with someone that I'm totally into, who's crazy about me!" My heart dropped as I knew he was not talking to me, but about me to his coworker. I hung up the phone and dialed back. When he picked up, I told him, "I heard what you said." He tried to cover, but I insisted that I knew what I heard. We agreed to meet after work to talk. I was stricken, hardly able to take care of my patient visits that day, feeling like I got kicked in the gut and was going to be sick.

We met at Twigs and sat outside. I didn't feel hungry, but hot and thirsty, and the wine went down easily. Paul explained how he was dissatisfied; I tried to make sense of why. I was devoted to him, made time for his needs, and we had celebrated our twenty-fifth anniversary two years earlier with an idyllic renewal of our vows on the beach. It made no sense to me. Paul left for a while as I sipped on wine and felt devastated. When he came back, I felt more than devastated.... I felt sick. I stumbled my way into the bathroom and promptly threw up all over the floor. I couldn't stand up; I felt so humiliated. He sent someone after me eventually, but I couldn't leave. Then Paul came to the door of the ladies' room and threatened me. He said I couldn't stay in there; the staff would call the police if I didn't get up. But I just curled in a ball on the floor and didn't answer, and he left.

Eventually I slunk out of the restaurant and into my car, moving it around the building to another area of the parking lot so he couldn't find me. I then stretched out on the front seat and slept.

Paul called me and left an angry message, telling me not to come home, that I was stupid for driving drunk and should be arrested. I wasn't *planning to drive any further than the parking lot and called my daughter. After explaining the argument, and my reluctance to drive, I told her I needed her to pick up my son from youth group. She agreed to this request, and another I made of her: "Please don't go home tonight. Take Caleb and go to a hotel for the night. Dad is angry." Ashley agreed and urged me to join them at the hotel.*

*But, after sleeping enough to feel sober, I drove home instead. Crazy, I know, but it seemed reasonable to me at the time. As I walked towards the front door, Paul met me with a shotgun and a duffle bag, yelling that I had five minutes to pack up some things and leave. I didn't feel scared, just determined that I wasn't leaving my own house for the crime of embarrassing him. Eventually, I was able to talk him down. He put the gun away, and I went into the house and stayed for the night. I even slept with him.*

*How did I get so low in my own estimation that I would not get myself to safety, not go to the hotel room with my children, and not listen to my daughter's pleas to leave that night?* **I had become the proverbial frog in the pot,** *living for years with someone who slowly turned up the heat through rejection and anger. I got accustomed to the temperature so when it was hot enough to kill me, I was completely numb to the danger. I didn't try to jump out of the relationship; I didn't react by standing up and yelling at Paul to stop.*

*The next morning, I met Jillian and Laurel at the tea shop. The pain and devastation were fresh, and I shared with my friends the details of the phone call, our meeting at Twigs, and my humiliation. I left out the part about the shotgun and the kids being sent to a hotel for the night. I wonder now whether omitting that part of the story was my way to keep from taking action to stop it.*

*My friends prayed for me and encouraged me to step-up my counseling appointments. I recall Laurel saying, "This is no way to live." This made me feel supported and understood, but I didn't know how to change it. I had ignored my feelings for so long that I continued to underreact to both emotional and physical danger.*

*My counselor and several books encouraged me to take a stand and change strategies when relating to Paul. I learned to stop being such a "nice Christian girl." Even Jesus took a harsh stance against wrong.*[37] *As I grew stronger and tolerated less, Paul distanced himself more. However, I read that, "It is imperative that you let go. When you let go you are admitting there is nothing you can do to change your difficult person."*[38] *Releasing Paul felt wrong, but Laurel and Jillian kept encouraging me that I was making wise and healthy choices. These choices were costly; there was backlash to my changes. Paul followed a textbook response of anger and "pulling away from me with a punishing silence."*[39]

---

"The best predictor of future behavior is past consistent behavior." Dr. Mary Dietzen

---

*Our relationship continued to unravel. He was angry more often and I felt a lot of anxiety. I tried to respond in healthy ways like not getting pulled into conflict, and acting lovingly even when I didn't feel like it. When he made another trip to the Ukraine, I left a letter in his suitcase telling him that I was letting him go. I loved him but I didn't want to try to make him love me back anymore. This made Paul angry enough to make an international call to let me know not to pick him up from the airport. He was moving out and would find another ride.*

*We met the evening after he returned, and he treated me with anger and scorn. The only thing we could agree on was to tell our kids that he was moving out. But the next day, in a last-minute change of heart, Paul decided he wanted to work on things. So, when we told our kids together, we explained that we were separating with the goal of working through our problems. They sat on the couch like they had years before, but responded differently, without emotion. We were all tired of the tension and conflict, and nobody begged him to stay.*

*Paul was to come back for his things on the weekend. The night before, I felt angry and anxious and didn't want to stay at home. What would it be*

*like to be there in the morning when he pulled up with the moving truck? I decided to spend the night with Laurel, and convinced my son, the only one at home, to join me. Neither one of us wanted the drama of watching Paul move out.*

*Paul called that night, wanting to get together for a drink. I refused; why would I want to socialize with him? He was moving out the next morning! Then he explained that he changed his mind, he didn't want to leave. I held my ground; we had told the kids we were separating. He needed to follow through. He was angry, and I was glad that Caleb and I were safe at Laurel's house.*

*That night it snowed, and Laurel and I woke to find footprints around my car, and a soggy note on my windshield. Paul had come looking for me in the night. When he couldn't find me at home, he guessed where I would be. But his attempt to convince me to back down was thwarted by the safety of my relationship with my friend, whose husband was a detective. Paul didn't even try to come in the house that night, and I was protected. I don't know how the story would have ended if I had stayed at home.*

*During the months we were separated, we met with different counselors and worked on our own issues. I made a list with my counselor of ten areas I needed to see progress in before we reunited. Gradually each one of those issues was addressed, and I felt guarded hope. After six months he moved back in.*

---

"On average, a person who leaves an abusive relationship will do so seven times before they make the final break" [40]

---

*We took a trip to Mexico, with our son, to celebrate. While waiting to be served in a lovely restaurant on the beach, Paul had a few drinks, grew impatient for the food, and decided we should leave. When we returned to the hotel, he lashed out at Caleb, saying it was a waste of money to bring him to Mexico since he just sat and watched TV. Paul lunged at him and hit him on the side of the face. I pulled on Paul, trying to keep him from Caleb, and he picked me up and threw me on the tile floor twice. The third time I tried to pull him away, he picked me up and took me to the bed and threw me on it, then stormed out.*

*I was so afraid. What would happen in Mexico if I called for help? How would they view domestic violence? I felt paralyzed. I checked on Caleb and saw he wasn't seriously harmed, and somehow, we went to bed. Paul stayed away for most of the night and slipped in sometime after I fell asleep. I recall awakening, and lying there, but not moving so he wouldn't know I was awake. The next morning, I got up early and paid our bill with my own money so Paul could never say he wasted his money on Caleb.*

*When Paul woke up, he apologized to both Caleb and me and expressed sorrow for his actions. He said he loved us and wanted to take us to breakfast. As we sat eating our breakfast, I felt nothing but self-contempt. I hated my weakness and powerlessness to stop the violence the night before. Later that day, I didn't want to sit next to him on the plane but behaved almost robotically to just get home.*

*The physical assault had the opposite effect on me than what I would have expected. Afterwards I didn't feel like making him move out; I felt I was not worth it, not worth protecting. Despite my best efforts to speak up, protect my heart, and stand up, nothing had changed. I couldn't even protect my son. When I described the incident later to my counselor, I was apathetic about Paul and very negative towards myself. The abuse was never reported to the authorities because it occurred in Mexico, and I never told anyone other than my counselor. He encouraged me to make a plan for safety, to set money aside, to pack a bag, and be ready to leave home at a moment's notice. We also worked together on setting boundaries around what I would tolerate at home, including Paul's drinking.*

---

"Abusers typically escalate when they feel they are losing control over the relationship, often because they feel that the independence of their partner has increased in some way or that their partner will leave. The escalation is not to be taken lightly-leaving an abusive relationship is a dangerous thing to do. In fact, 75% of all serious injuries in abusive relationships occur when the survivor ends the relationship." [41]

---

*The next time Paul physically abused me was directly related to me holding a boundary, of not being pulled into conflict. He was in the mood for a fight, and jabbing at me verbally, so I went to bed with a book to avoid him. He came in the room after me, continuing to try to start an argument, and I calmly told him, "I don't have anything to say to you right now." That was enough to make him silence me by sitting on top of me, with his knees pinning my arms down and his hands around my throat, choking me. I couldn't get any air, and really thought he was going to kill me. When he let go, I felt so defeated and worthless that I didn't try to stop him when he approached me for sex. I knew he was sick, and I felt sick too. The next morning, there were bruises on my chest and back from where he sat on me, and my throat hurt with every swallow from him choking me. He had succeeded in quieting me that night, and I hated myself more than I hated him.*

# 8

# Keys to Healing

Cinderella's healing and transformation took place
**one layer at a time.**

The **first layer** addressed her **value.** Thanks to her fairy
godmother, Cinderella's makeover and magical gown had given
a boost to her self-esteem. She approached the prince with
confidence, and in time, embraced her new identity as "the one
the prince loved."

Embracing her value, she was now ready to face the difficult truth
about her past. The **second layer of healing** took place when the
stepmother locked Cinderella in her bedroom. This **isolation**
allowed her to see her past, her family, and her abuse **objectively**.
It was a painful experience, but her **friends** aided the process by
bringing her the **keys that led to her freedom!**

# Key #1: FACE WHAT YOU'RE TRYING SO HARD TO FORGET

## 8.1 Worsening PTSD

I felt defeated. For over a year, I had done my best to weather the family backlash that resulted from the revelation of sexual abuse by my father. What I wanted, the time and space to pursue healing without my dad's interference, finally came, but only after I cut all ties with both my parents.

The grief over the loss of relationship with my mom in particular was profound. Despite the many ways she had disappointed me, I desperately wanted her in my life.

This loss only compounded the escalating emotional problems I was having. Depression, anxiety, and trouble with intimacy had gotten much worse during the previous year. In addition, I was now having other symptoms of PTSD like flashbacks and nightmares of being attacked. It was not uncommon for my husband's sleep to be interrupted by my screams for help.

Not surprisingly, my emotional crisis made going to work a real challenge. I wanted to stay home, but those days when I did stay home were actually my lowest. Left alone with my own thoughts, my uninterrupted hours of grief only made matters worse.

I found my best days were when I got out of the house. Responsibilities, meetings, and being around others gave me a reprieve. However, being at work was not easy. Circumstances and people sometimes served as triggers to surface past trauma.

## 8.2 Am I Going Crazy?

"It isn't that big a deal," I told myself at work one day after reading an email from my senior pastor. Although we had been scheduled to meet that afternoon, he had to cancel. It was becoming a common occurrence and coincided with Stan's promotion to Executive Pastor. I didn't like it, but I knew it was reasonable.

Later that afternoon, as I sat in my office with the door open, I saw my senior pastor go into Stan's office and shut the door. Immediately, I was disrupted. I tried to refocus on the work in front of me but seemed unable to concentrate. I had a strange desire to run and thought about going home. But it was only two p.m. How would I explain it? I decided to stay.

However, over the course of the next hour, as the sound of their muffled voices drifted through our shared office wall, I became highly emotional. I cried but had no idea why. I felt afraid but wasn't sure what I was afraid of. I felt dread, as if something bad was about to happen.

Somehow, I willed myself to stay put until four p.m., an acceptable time to leave for home. Walking across the parking lot, I was quite sure I was going crazy. Where was this going to end? How much worse was it going to get? The flashbacks, the panic attacks, the unexplained fear and dread... I contemplated what it would be like to admit myself to the psych ward and wondered if that wasn't where this whole thing was headed.

## 8.3 Recalling Repressed Memories

My emotional instability and worsening condition led me to consider counseling with Walter again. It was obvious that my senior pastor and Stan's relationship was a trigger surfacing something traumatic from my past. With my husband and Janis's blessing, I made an appointment and resumed the work started over thirteen months earlier.

As I closed my eyes in Walter's office, I could hear a child's voice in my head. "Daddy is mean and cruel; he hurts me and talks bad. I don't want daddy to love me. He's creepy." I paused, and looked up at Walter, and repeated to him what had come to mind.

"Little Laurel," he said, "wants to tell you what happened. She's still back there, carrying the memory of what took place. When the abuse occurred, she protected you by interacting with your dad, so you didn't have to."

"Children dissociate during abuse... The abusive act is too painful or too frightening for you to experience. All feelings are blocked; you 'go away.' You are disconnected from the act, the perpetrator, and yourself." [42]

Can I just stop here and tell you that this was an incredibly difficult concept for me to embrace? Put on the twilight zone music and roll the tape! Was this really happening?

As Walter described how repression works in language I could accept, it began to make sense. To live with my dad while I was experiencing severe abuse, I dissociated. Part of me experienced the abuse, and part of me didn't. One of the goals of the work we were about to do, was to bring these two parts of myself together. The way to do that? Talk to Little Laurel, listen to what happened, and allow God's Spirit to help me face the truth.

This discussion led me to ask the question, "So do I have multiple personality disorder?" (Dissociative Identity Disorder or DID) "No," Walter said. "If that was the case, different parts of you would be emerging in your life now. For instance, you might 'go away' during the day, while another personality steps in. There would be unexplained events and gaps in your waking life. Like maybe you would find yourself at the park one afternoon and not remember how you got there."

"Do you feel you can talk to Little Laurel and ask her what she wants to tell you?" I wanted to say "No," but instead gave it a try. The result was that I both heard and saw something that happened when I was about five years old. My dad, my brother Brett, and I were in the kitchen watching my mom pull out of the driveway. Dad was in his work clothes and had come home to watch us kids so my mom could go to the grocery store. He seemed angry about it, and once she was out of sight, began undoing the zipper of his pants. I watched in my mind, as he sat down on a chair in the kitchen, removed my underwear, and pulled me onto his lap. Suddenly I felt a tremendous amount of pain and started to cry and squirm. "I told you to sit still!" he said and then began to rape me. I could see the anxiety, confusion, and panic I experienced as a little girl during the event. I cried, screamed, and asked him to stop but he didn't. When it was over, he stood up, and yelled, "Stop crying, that didn't hurt you."

As the memory unfolded, I was surprisingly calm, like it was happening to someone else. This made it hard to believe it really happened. I prayed and asked God to confirm the memory was real. Immediately I saw in prayer an image of a drop of blood falling onto the kitchen floor, recalling its avocado green pattern as it did. I hadn't seen that floor in over thirty-five years.

## 8.4 Why Go Back and Dig Up the Past?

Recalling the rape revealed that the nature of the sexual abuse became very violent. At the same time my parents added a baby boy to our family. Brett was carefully chosen, hand-picked, and adored. Stan's transfer, favor, and promotion reminded me of Brett's adoption and the subsequent change in relationship with my dad. My struggles at work started to make a lot of sense.

Prior to Stan's hire, I enjoyed my job. I was entrusted with difficult assignments and thrived. However, after Stan was hired, I was passed over for a promotion. Experiences at work, like moving out of my office and giving it to him, triggered these memories from my childhood. It was like Stan was "adopted," and in my mind, he was the "boy" my pastor and his wife always wanted. Consequently, I was anxious and hypervigilant, waiting for and expecting an attack like those I had experienced from my dad after Brett's adoption.

My question, "Do I really have to go back and recall more of the memories of abuse to get better?" was answered with a resounding "Yes!" This truth is widely accepted in a variety of clinical settings for victims of domestic violence, rape, and even veterans returning from combat.

I learned this after watching an episode of 60 minutes about Advanced PTSD Therapy. During the episode, several soldiers described emotions that had derailed their life: depression, anger, extreme anxiety, inability to sleep, avoidance, hypervigilance, irritability, nightmares, sense of worthlessness, and guilt. It was easy to see that these soldiers and I had a lot in common. Although our trauma came from different sources, we were experiencing many of the same symptoms.

Surprisingly, the show included a scene that reminded me of one of my sessions with Walter. A soldier sat with his therapist, closed his eyes, and forced himself to recall out loud a traumatic event from his past. However, the solider did this not once, but five times! Many of the soldiers interviewed saw improvement in their PTSD symptoms as a result of repeating every detail of the events they were trying so hard to forget.[43]

I believe you can't be healed of something you deny ever happened. It's not easy, but running towards the traumatic memories of the past, and incorporating them into your story, sets you on the path towards healing.

## 8.5 Disturbing Dreams

Convinced I was on the right track, I found the courage to make another appointment with Walter. The week prior, I had a strange but very vivid dream. In it, I was with my siblings, Brett and Debbie. We were playing outside, when a large bear charged towards us. Anticipating the attack, I told Brett and Debbie to lay down, and covered them with a blanket. Then, I turned to face the bear, who overtook me.

---

"Repressed memory dreams are dreams that contain a partial repressed memory or symbols that provide access to a repressed memory." [44]

---

After the dream, I wondered if the dream was significant, and if the bear was my dad. That suspicion was confirmed in my next visit with Walter. As I closed my eyes, the image of the bedroom my sister and I shared in early elementary school came to mind. I was playing, when my dad appeared at the doorway. I heard Little Laurel's voice in my mind say, "I can't get away."

Then the memory of what happened began to unfold in my mind. My dad told me get on the bed. When I said "No, I don't want to," his anger erupted. "You don't tell me what you're going to do! I said get on the bed and spread your legs!" The image of myself frozen in place was followed by my dad's voice, "Where is Debbie? Do you want me to go get her?" Thoughts like, "He hates me," followed by, "Better me than her," came to mind, as I watched the attack play out in my mind. He forced himself on me, his anger escalating even further, and as I resisted, he screamed, "You're going to pay for this! Worthless!"

As I recalled the incident in Walter's office, something very strange happened. My body responded by "remembering" it as well. Walter had warned me of this phenomenon on a previous visit, but I was surprised nonetheless. I could feel vaginal pressure and discomfort even though nothing was happening to me physically at the time.

As we concluded our session that day, Walter told me that threatening to hurt a sibling was a common strategy used by sexual offenders. I thought about the nightmare I had prior to the visit, and felt confident God was preparing me in advance to believe the recollection was true.

## 8.6 Did This Really Happen?

Between sessions with Walter, I was often plagued with doubts and fear. Fear of being wrong. I wondered if it was possible to make this kind of thing up. It was in those moments of doubt, that I got out the list of all the supporting facts I believed gave credibility to my surfacing memories of abuse.

What was on the list?

- The body memory I had experienced my whole life. Those random episodes of phantom pressure, pain, and discomfort in my mouth were classic symptoms of sexual abuse. I knew I didn't make that up.

- My dad laughed when I was sexually assaulted as a teenager while working at the restaurant. In the book, *Repressed Memories*, the author wrote this was a stereotypical response by predators.[45]
- Sexual abuse runs in families. My dad confessed he had been sexually abused. My uncle also exposed himself and tried to lure me into having sex with him when I was very young.
- My mom's initial reaction when she learned I was in counseling for some things in my childhood was to say, "Was it your dad? I don't doubt it." I believed this supported she had suspected something was wrong.
- My parents' far-fetched arguments that my dad couldn't have abused me actually gave my recollections credibility. "I was never alone with Laurel her entire childhood." "I am not circumcised." And the worst of all, "Why would I have abused Laurel when I had a handicap daughter that would have enjoyed it?"
- My dad's lies. For over a year, I heard family repeat things my dad said about me that were not true. Why? Why lie if you aren't guilty of something?
- My dad's refusal to talk about the past. Why? What was he afraid of?

This list of supporting evidence grew over time. One morning, I was home alone, when a conversation that had always puzzled me came to mind. It had been years since I had thought about the day my mom and I were in the kitchen together. She had all the clean laundry out on the table, and was busy sorting, folding, and ironing. As she worked, she said in a rather matter of fact tone, "I don't know what happened between you and your dad. You used to be so close. In fact, sometimes I was jealous of the two of you."

I remember even as a little girl, being perplexed by her observation. I thought to myself, "I was close with my dad? I don't remember that." At the time, I didn't have any fond memories of him. Now, as an adult, it suddenly made sense! My mom had noticed the change in our relationship that took place when I started to refuse my dad's requests for sex.

Instantly, I felt sick! I started to heave, ran to the kitchen sink, and threw up. Just then, the doorbell rang. It was Marci. "God told me to come," she said as she hugged me. Sobbing, I put my head on my dear friend's shoulder. I was overcome, not just by the memory, but also with how much God loved me. He knew ahead of time the kind of day I was going to have, and he knew just who to send to help me through it.

I was very blessed to be a part of a community of people who loved me. I was never without the support I needed because I had Mike, my kids, girlfriends, and a large church family. The entire time I was in treatment, I kept attending the two small groups I was in and confided openly about what I was going through. Many times, God used timely help from my friends to get me through this horrific season in my life.

## 8.7 Family Secrets

As in many cases of incest, I was abused by more than one family member. The memory of this event started to emerge while shopping one day. It was so odd. I was looking at bedding, when out of nowhere, I saw an image drop down in front of my eyes and then disappear immediately afterwards. The image was a little girl, from the neck down, wearing a yellow dress, white anklets, and white patent leather shoes. There one second, gone the next, the mental picture was accompanied by the thought, "I can't think of that right now."

It took me a minute, but I composed myself, started down the store isle, then was surprised by it again. This time, I grabbed onto a shelf full of sale items as a wave of nausea swept over me. What was going on?

I left my cart, and went to my car, concluding that the flashback must be linked to another traumatic event in my childhood. My mom and I were still on speaking terms at the time, and I mentioned the yellow dress to her during a phone call. Her response was quite shocking. She said, "Oh I remember that yellow dress. You wore it when you were a flower girl at your aunt and uncle's wedding. You looked so pretty that day. I was really worried about you."

When I questioned why she would be worried, she changed the subject. Although troubling, I didn't explore the image with Walter until after I was estranged from my mom, when it surfaced again in one of our sessions. I was about seven years old, when my aunt and uncle, my dad's oldest stepbrother, asked me to be the flower girl in their wedding. I remember looking forward to the special event. My mom made my dress, and on the day of the wedding, a hairstylist fixed my hair in a very pretty and grown-up looking "up-do." I even had my own bouquet of flowers to carry during the ceremony. Afterwards, the reception was held at my dad's father's house.

Looking down on the event as it unfolded in my mind, I could see myself, in the basement where my grandfather and others were gathered drinking and playing pool. As I watched my grandpa contemplate his next shot, a glass of whiskey rested on the edge of the table.

---

"Viewing the scene from up above, or some other out-of-body perspective is common among sexual abuse survivors." [46]

---

Suddenly, this image was gone, and another took its place. I was in my uncle's bedroom, also in the basement. Someone was on top of me. It wasn't my dad, but another member of his family. I was struggling, kicking and pushing him away, and during the struggle I received a blow to my face.

"Uncross your legs, you stupid little bitch!" he said. I tried screaming; he placed his hand over my mouth and said, "Shut up if you know what's good for you!" From inside me came the knowledge that I was in a lot of physical pain. After it was over, I emerged from the bedroom with a bloody nose crying, my beautiful up-do disheveled, and my dress stained with blood.

## 8.8 How Do I Handle All This Anger?

As I reflected on the painful memory, I couldn't help but wonder how my mom could not have noticed I had been sexually assaulted. There must have been physical trauma, bruises, blood and other evidence. Did she suspect but decide she "couldn't face it?" Isn't that what she had been telling me all year?

The notion made me angry, very angry. I felt abandoned by my mom and the pain of her betrayal felt like a knife stabbing me in the heart.

This was not the first time I had wrestled with feelings of pain and anger towards her. Many times, I perceived her inaction, lies, and defense of my dad as a betrayal.

In a session with Janis, we talked about my emerging anger. I had no idea what to do with it. We were estranged, not on speaking terms, and talking to her about what I was recalling was out of the question. However, Janis encouraged me to write a letter to my mom. "Don't hold back" she said. "Tell her exactly how you feel. But when you're done, don't mail it. Tear it up and throw it away."

I did this exercise not once, but on many occasions and it proved to be very helpful.

## 8.9 How Long Did It Go On?

As I continued to recall memories of being sexually abused by my dad it became clear that my sister had also been a victim. Although my dad's statement to Mike the year before hinted that she "would enjoy" such encounters, my recollections told quite a different story. Debbie cried, was afraid, and on multiple occasions I tried to intervene on her behalf. This did not fare well for me of course. My dad retaliated with physical violence and would strike me or pick me up and throw me down onto the floor.

For this reason, I realized how fortunate it was that Debbie had moved out of the house at the age of twelve. Living at Lakeland Village had spared her further abuse. I, however, was not so fortunate.

By the time Debbie moved out, my bedroom had been moved to the basement. It was there that my dad sometimes came to visit me in the middle of the night. His footsteps on the stairs were often my first clue of what was to come. I thought about running, but where would I go? How could I get away?

The abuse continued until I was sixteen and in high school. This was the last memory I recalled and the hardest attack to accept. Somehow the fact I was older and fully developed, made me feel dirtier. I know I tried to fight him off, but I still blamed myself for allowing it to happen. Did I do enough?

For the first time, I wished I hadn't repressed the abuse. If only I had reported him! He could have gone to jail for what he had done to me! But, no, he got away with it. Again, I was plagued with feelings of injustice, anger, and even hatred. I vented these feelings in the same way I had done with my mom, in letters. Letters I would have loved to mail but didn't. Instead I tore them up, symbolically releasing the offense as I did.

## KEY #2: DISCOVER HOW IT AFFECTED YOU

Facing what I was trying so hard to forget was the first step in my healing. Dealing with the damage it caused was the next.

In my sessions with Walter and Janis we spent a lot of time discovering and discussing how the abuse I suffered affected me. It wasn't easy, it took courage, but acknowledging the pain I experienced, lies I believed, and unhealthy ways I coped, put me in a position for God to heal me.

### 8.10   Draining Out the Pain

One of my mentors through the years has been Joyce Meyers. Although I've never met her in person, she's taught me a lot about emotional healing through her writing and teaching ministry.

Joyce often says, "Feelings buried alive never die." I discovered this was true for me. Every time I looked and spoke about a traumatic memory, the emotional pain I buried when it happened spilled out. As I have already said, there were many tears and I was profoundly sad, sometimes for weeks at a time. But revealing my pain was HEALTHY!

However, as healthy as it was, when I was experiencing the pain, I felt like I was regressing, not moving forward. I often vented my frustrations to others saying, "I should never have gone to counseling; I am worse not better!" However, I realize now that my pain had a purpose.

I like to compare the process I went through to how you treat a deep tissue wound. I guess that's the nurse in me. In the hospital, if a wound became infected, we reopened, drained, and cleansed the wound daily. This was an incredibly painful procedure for the patient, but it resulted in the wound healing from the inside out.

Likewise, in my situation, when a memory was reopened, what drained out was pain, shame, and usually a lie, either a false belief about myself, or about God. As I brought those things to Jesus in prayer, He cleansed me, and I was supernaturally healed from the inside out.

## 8.11 How Do I Face People?

Like most other victims, I experienced overwhelming shame as the truth about my past emerged. I worried about what others thought about me, especially those close to my parents, and avoided relationship with them as a result.

However, when my grandma, my mom's mom, became gravely ill, Mike and I decided to make the four-hour trip to say goodbye, despite the fact other family members would be there. When we got to the hospital, my mom's two sisters, their husbands, and my cousins were all congregated around my grandma's bed. I was so glad to see them, but at the same time felt an incredible amount of shame. I had no idea how they felt about me or the conflict with my parents. Did they think I was crazy? Did they believe the polygraph results and my dad's claim he was innocent? Or did they believe it happened? Did they see me as damaged goods?

I did my best to hold my head up and keep a smile on my face, but when they all decided to go get something to eat, I saw it as an opportunity to be alone. "I'm not hungry," I said, "I'll just stay here with grandma." My uncle chimed in, "I'm going to stay too."

After everyone left, he asked me how I was doing. At first, I gave him a very polite answer. "I'm good." But when he pressed for something more authentic, I responded in kind and confessed I was overwhelmed with shame.

"Why do you feel shame?" he asked, adding, "That's surprising, it obviously wasn't your fault." He had a good point. Why did I? It took some digging, but what I learned is that my shame was rooted in lies.

Acknowledging I had participated in heinous sexual acts with my own father resulted in a painful feeling of wrongdoing. It didn't seem to matter to me that I had been lured, groomed, or even forced into it.

In fact, the mere idea I had been a victim compounded the shame I felt. As a victim, I felt weak, overpowered, and insignificant. Obviously, I wasn't worth much.

It was shame, more than any other feeling, that made me want to die. So many times, I wanted out. This temptation didn't go away until I connected the shame with the lie that was fueling it.

Following are some of the lies that I believed.

## 8.12 Lie: It Was My Fault

Shocking isn't it? But, like other childhood victims of sexual abuse, I believed that what happened to me was my fault.

In one of my first appointments with Janis, I told her, "I feel so dirty." I just couldn't shake the image of that little toddler enjoying having sex with her own father. The self-contempt was almost unbearable. She responded, "So, is that what you would tell Kelsey?" Confused by what my daughter had to do with it, I asked, "What do you mean?" Janis proceeded, "If Kelsey came to you and said she had been sexually abused, would you say, "You are so dirty?" The notion seemed absurd to me and I easily understood the point she was trying to make. "No," I said. And she asked, "Then why would you heap that shame on yourself?"

I couldn't help but think about my dad's words to me when I tried to resist his sexual advances. Statements like, "You are going to pay for this," and "Worthless." His words reinforced what I already believed, that there was something wrong with me.

In the course of my treatment, I learned to recognize shame as a feeling that was completely inappropriate. I took it off like I would a piece of clothing, refusing to wear something that didn't fit my situation. Instead, I visually imagined myself placing the shame and guilt where it belonged, with my dad.

The lie, "it was my fault" had to be replaced with the truth, **"I did nothing to deserve what happened to me."**

## 8.13 Lie: I'm Needed, Not Wanted

I have always felt needed. I was needed to care for my sister Debbie at a very young age. I liked doing this and was very involved in her care until she died. However, both parents relied on me in other ways that were very unhealthy. My mom needed me to be her friend, helping her cope with my dad when I was a teenager and on into adulthood. My dad needed me to bear the brunt of his sexual assaults and anger. I was his scapegoat, blamed for much of the family dysfunction.

Although I was needed, the idea that my parents were "given me, but wanted something else" surfaced. As a result, I believed I was a disappointment.

In my family of origin, I felt validated for what I did, not who I was. Consequently, to get approval, love and attention, I worked hard to do things that were needed and do them well. This served me well in sports, my nursing career, and in ministry. My hard work often reaped benefits of affirmation and appreciation. However, my performance-driven mentality had its down-sides. Like the negative feelings I had towards myself if I failed or underperformed. Others have often told me that I am "hard on myself."

Uncovering the lie, **needed, but not wanted**, was a key to my healing. It explained the triggers at work, my need to perform and the devastation

I felt when I failed at something. It also explained why I had trouble trusting that others valued me, especially others in authority.

This realization was half the battle to change. The other half was simply applying the truth, **I am both needed and wanted**. I practiced giving people the benefit of the doubt. I assumed that others did want me, and that the relationship didn't hinge on what I could do for them.

### 8.14 Lie: I'm Always in Trouble

During the years I was struggling with PTSD, a new lie emerged. I would awaken in the morning, plagued with fear that I was "in trouble." This made facing the day rather difficult. I felt dread of what was coming, afraid that whatever I had done was going to have severe consequences.

In phone conversations with Lynn and Jillian, I would confess my belief I had done something wrong but couldn't explain why. I would just say, "I feel like I am in trouble." Although my friends would say, "this doesn't seem to fit," I couldn't seem to shake the fear.

Eventually, I connected this belief to my childhood. As I recalled the memories of sexual abuse, I realized that I often had no warning or rationale for why I was hurt, scorned, or mistreated. As a child, I assumed that the pain inflicted was a consequence for my behavior. I lived in fear of making a mistake and what the penalties were going to be.

As a result, I became a perfectionist. I had high standards for myself, and if they were not met, I was sure that God, like my dad, was upset with me.

Again, recognizing the lie was half the battle. I knew the truth from the Bible, that I was forgiven of my past, present and future sins. However, applying it to myself was the challenge. Giving myself grace, permission to screw up, and believing God was not mad at me took time and practice. I began to exchange the lie, *I'm always in trouble,* for **the truth, I do not have to be perfect; I am forgiven.**

## 8.15 Lie: God Didn't Protect Me

In one of my early sessions with Walter, after recalling a painful incident of sexual abuse, Walter asked me "Where do you think God was when this was happening to you?" Honestly, I had never thought about it. "I don't know," I said. Walter responded, "Let's ask Him to show you."

As we bowed our heads to pray, what came to mind was alarming. A scene emerged. I was with my dad, who was approaching me with the obvious intent to hurt me. Suddenly, I saw Jesus. He began pleading with my dad to stop. His words: "This is my child, stop hurting her." But my dad didn't stop. And, as I cried out for help, Jesus reassured me He was there, and wouldn't leave.

Initially, I did not find this revelation of God's presence during my abuse comforting. Instead I felt abandoned. I went home angry and hurt that God had stood by and allowed the abuse to happen. Why didn't God protect me?

I believe that God is good. He loves us with a perfect love. When we hurt, so does He. On one hand, I believed God didn't approve of what my dad did to me. But on the other hand, I also knew God had the power to stop him. So, why hadn't He? What about all those verses in the Bible about protection?

My questions led me to study these verses. I discovered that many times, the original word used meant, "keep you," not protect. For example, Numbers 6:24, "The Lord Bless you, and keep you"[47] has been revised in many translations to read, "May the Lord bless you and protect you."[48] The difference is subtle. But, when God promises to "keep" us, He is not guaranteeing protection from all suffering. Rather, He promises to keep us as we endure suffering of any kind.

Had God kept me during the abuse? Yes! In my case, God kept me by repressing the memory of the abuse until I had the maturity and support to face it.

**Truth: God was with me and helped me get through it**. The truth was that God's presence helped me survive the experience. And even if I had not survived physically, my soul would have been preserved. I knew Jesus and had placed my trust in Him as my Savior at a young age. Nothing my earthly father did to me could have changed that.

## 8.16 Unhealthy Ways I Coped

I would love to tell you that I recovered from being sexually abused as a child by simply relying on God, but that would not be true. The truth is that sometimes I turned to other things to relieve the pain; things like food and alcohol.

Food is easier to talk about. Let's start there. Food has always been something I turned to for comfort. I remember the beginning of my ninth-grade year, attending a dance at my high school. I sat on the sidelines of the gymnasium the entire night; not one single person asked me to dance. By the time I got home I felt undesirable and went straight to the refrigerator to make myself feel better. I poured myself a big bowl of cereal and ate it before going to bed. Ever since then, I have been tempted to eat when I'm upset.

In the years leading up to and while in counseling, I gained thirty to forty pounds. It was embarrassing to say the least. Food was comforting, but in no way provided an "escape" from the horrible images that were surfacing in counseling, flashbacks, and nightmares. For that, I would need a stronger "medication." I'll never forget, sitting on the couch one day, telling my husband, "I just want to get drunk." He responded with, "No, we're not going to do that."

Excessive alcohol consumption had never been a temptation. That is, until I discovered the benefits of having alcohol in my system before being intimate with Mike. After a couple glasses of wine, it was easier to relax, not freeze up physically when touched, and push the memories of being attacked by my dad out of my mind.

I knew it was unhealthy and felt guilty for drinking. I would make a commitment to stop, and then fail when sex proved to be too hard without it. But numbing my senses was keeping me from getting better. I eventually got rid of my "crutch," which forced Mike and I to come up with other ways to help me relax. Things like backrubs and focusing on

Mike by keeping my eyes open, made it easier to reject invading images. Mike also began talking to me during our time together. Hearing his voice kept me in the present, and less likely to reflect on previous trauma.

It has taken years to undo the damage that was done in this area of my life. Intimacy with my husband was probably the most difficult area of my recovery, and the slowest to heal. Thankfully, new memories have started to replace the old, and sexual intimacy has gotten easier.

# KEY #3 EMBRACE THE STRUGGLE

## 8.17 Resist the Temptation to Run

For a long period, both before and after my memories resurfaced, I had an overwhelming desire to quit my job. My work environment triggered strong emotions, and I was often tempted to submit my letter of resignation. I actually wrote it several times! I knew that quitting would bring quick relief to the overwhelming symptoms of PTSD. But remaining in that uncomfortable place, not running, was a key to my healing.

Separation from my parents was necessary for me to make progress. However, staying in what felt like similar circumstances at work allowed me to struggle through a replay of my childhood with safe people, and experience a different outcome. The struggle itself was part of my healing.

Like a butterfly experiences transformation while isolated in the cocoon, I changed during the separation from my folks. Facing the truth and then allowing God to heal me from the inside out resulted in behavioral changes others began to notice.

I responded to rejection differently. Rejection still stung, but it no longer overwhelmed me emotionally. I wasn't incapacitated by it. In fact, sometimes my reaction was so minimal, I wondered if the pendulum hadn't swung a little too far to the other side.

Other changes were evident as well. The anxiety attacks and fear of the future were things of the past. I wasn't bracing myself for what was around the next corner anymore. My fear of making mistakes and facing the consequences lessened, and I found it easier to accept God's grace and mercy. Instead of perfectionistic, the expectations I had for myself were more realistic.

Although I was still a work in progress, clearly, I was not in crisis anymore. I believed I had changed. With new strength emerging, an opportunity to test and ultimately reinforce those changes presented itself.

## 8.18 A New Family Picture

In one of my early appointments with Janis, she painted a picture of what a future relationship with my parents could look like. She said, "When you're healed, you'll be able to see and spend time with your mom and dad. Since it is unlikely your dad will admit to what he did, it won't be a close relationship. But one day, you'll be able to have them over to your house, spend a few hours together, and be perfectly fine doing so."

At the time this conversation occurred, shortly after the first revelation of sexual abuse, I couldn't believe my ears. I was so afraid of my dad that I couldn't picture ever seeing him again. I thought surely, she had to be joking and told her so. But Janis reassured me this was our goal.

As it turned out, Janis's coaching was spot on! Reengaging my dad in relationship, after a period of separation, would prove to be good for me. Facing him would make me even stronger.

I came across an illustration I found tremendously helpful during this challenging time. Whenever I questioned why God would let me struggle for so long, I thought about this story:

> Once a little boy was playing outdoors and found a fascinating caterpillar. He carefully picked it up and took it home to show his mother. He asked his mother if he could keep it, and she said he could if he would take good care of it.
>
> The little boy got a large jar from his mother and put plants for food, and a climbing stick in the jar. Every day he watched the caterpillar and brought it new plants to eat. One day the caterpillar climbed up the stick and started acting strangely. The boy worriedly called his mother who came and saw that the caterpillar was creating a cocoon.

*The mother explained to her son how the caterpillar was going to go through a metamorphosis and become a butterfly.*

*The little boy was thrilled to hear about the changes his caterpillar would go through. He watched every day, waiting for the butterfly to emerge. One day it happened, a small hole appeared in the cocoon and the butterfly started to struggle to come out.*

*At first the boy was excited, but soon he became concerned. The butterfly was struggling so hard to get out! It looked like it couldn't break free! It looked desperate! It looked like it was making no progress!*

*The boy was so concerned he decided to help. He ran to get scissors, and then walked back (because he had learned not to run with scissors). He snipped the cocoon to make the hole bigger and the butterfly quickly emerged.*

*As the butterfly came out the boy was surprised. It had a swollen body and small, shriveled wings. He continued to watch the butterfly expecting that, at any moment, the wings would dry out, enlarge and expand to support the swollen body. He knew that in time the body would shrink, and the butterfly's wings would expand. But neither happened!*

*The butterfly spent the rest of its life crawling around with a swollen body and shriveled wings. It never was able to fly...*

*As the boy tried to figure out what had gone wrong, his mother took him to talk to a biologist from a local college. There, her son learned that the butterfly was **SUPPOSED** to struggle. In fact, the butterfly's struggle to push its way through the tiny opening of the cocoon pushes the fluid out of its body and into its wings. Without the struggle, the butterfly would never, ever fly. The boy's good intentions hurt the butterfly.*

*As you go through school, and life, keep in mind that struggling is an important part of any growth experience. In fact, it is the struggle that causes you to develop your ability to fly.[49]*

As a result of this article, I came to appreciate God's plan for my recovery. He didn't remove my struggles at work or with my parents because He wanted me to learn to fly!

<><><><><><><><><><><><><><> # Jillian <><><><><><><><><><><><><><><>

## Behind Closed Doors—A Shocking Revelation

*After facing the truth about my abortion, I felt free and hoped this freedom would improve my relationship with Jacob. It did not improve. Life went on and I accepted Jacob's excuses of complacency along with his profession of love for me. I had a desire since childhood to be loved and cherished. I was counting on Jacob to fulfill that desire.*

*My granddaughters often came over to spend the weekend with us. Saturday morning, I was normally out on the porch having coffee about 6:30 a.m. The girls would wake up one by one and join me. We would chat and listen to the birds sing. But this particular morning, I slept in. The girls were up before me watching TV with Jacob in the living room.*

*I leaned over to kiss Jacob's cheek and saw his face was flushed. I put my hand on his leg to hold his hand. As I did so, my arm brushed against his groin. I noticed he had an erection. I knew I wasn't the one who had ex-cited him. When I asked him to follow me into the kitchen and confronted him with my discovery, he turned red. The next words he spoke sent me reeling. He admitted he was looking at one of the girls and got aroused. I stood there in shock. I could not wrap my mind around what he just said. My granddaughter??? You were sexually aroused from just looking at MY GRANDDAUGHTER???*

*He said he was sorry. I stood there by the kitchen sink in shock. I de-manded he leave the house immediately. He wanted to hug me and say he was sorry. I refused to let him come near me and said we would talk later. He hung his head, gave me a sad puppy look, and walked out the back door.*

*The girls were asking where he went when I returned to the living room. I made up an excuse that one of the cows might be out, so he had to leave in a hurry. I said I was surprising them and taking them out to breakfast before they had to go home. We got ready and left. Trying to act like nothing was wrong, I barely got through breakfast. It was the only time I wanted to take them home sooner rather than later. I dropped them off and drove away with tears streaming down my cheeks. My heart was heavy as the thought of confronting Jacob weighed me down.*

---

"An estimated 20 percent of American children have been sexually molested. Offenders are usually family friends or relatives. Types of activities vary and may include just looking at a child or undressing and touching a child." [50]

---

*I stayed away from home, trying to figure out what I was going to do. I prayed and asked God for wisdom. My friendship with Lynn and Laurel had deepened so much that we were more like sisters than friends. I called them, shared my crisis and asked them to pray. I wanted to run away and not come back. I contemplated moving out. Lynn and Laurel wondered why I should be the one to move. Jacob was the one in the wrong. If I left, I would have the responsibility of finding a place to stay and being inconvenienced. He would have all the comforts of being home. It made sense to ask him to move out. I went to a hotel for the night to make a plan for how to deliver the news.*

*When I got home the next day, Jacob was waiting for me. He told me how sorry he was for hurting me. Tears pooled in his eyes. As if his confession of being aroused by my granddaughter wasn't enough, there was more. He wanted to come clean. He admitted that he didn't need to look at pictures anymore, he could just visualize them whenever he wanted to be aroused. The more he fantasized, the more it took to get him excited. That was his excuse for his attraction to young girls.*

*While I stood there in shock and disbelief, he cried and kept on confessing. I wanted to vomit but it was stuck in my throat. Supposedly, con-*

fession is good for the soul. Jacob was relieved to share his dark secrets, but now I felt the weight of his shame, damaging my own heart. I began to see the real reason why his eyes were glazed over when we were intimate. He wasn't with me. He was with the fantasies in his mind.

I should have stopped him, but he kept on spilling his guts, interjected with how sorry he was. He ended his confession with, "I don't blame you if you want a divorce. I will take full responsibility." I yelled, referring to his fantasies, "HOW COULD YOU EVEN THINK OF DOING WHAT YOU DO? THIS IS CRAZY!!" Then what I said next still shocks me. I told him he wasn't going to get off that easy. Instead of taking him up on his offer of divorce, I told him he HAD to get help. True to my pattern of handling life, I bypassed my feelings and pushed down my anger. There was no letting it sink in or it would sink me.

---

"Characteristics of pedophiles: obsessive, problems in current relationships, emotionally immature, depressed, insecure, and controlling." Dr. Mary Dietzen

---

I felt trapped by my vow to marry Jacob for better or for worse. My mind immediately focused on trying to solve how we would survive this. Jacob needed to move out, but I wasn't ready to completely give up on our relationship. Maybe he could get well. I convinced myself that I needed to make this marriage work.

During our separation, I found a counselor and went to her weekly. Jacob joined a sexual addiction men's group and I joined one for spouses. When other wives shared, I felt their husbands' addictions were mild in comparison to mine. Shame about Jacob's attraction to young girls kept me from sharing my story. Week after week, I would do the homework in the workbook, attend the meetings, listen to the other wives, and go home carrying the same secret I brought with me.

Jacob found out about a counseling organization for sex addicts called

*Heart to Heart. After hearing they offered intensives for couples on the brink of divorce, he called me and asked if I would go with him to Colorado. This request came as a surprise to me. After all, he was the man who hated to spend an extra dollar on crackers. He told me he had taken in truckloads of scrap metal laying around the farm to pay for the trip and the counseling costs. I was impressed he would make such an effort. I had spent years begging him to clean up the junk outside. Here he was doing it and investing the money to try and salvage our marriage. I agreed to go with the stipulation he would book me a separate room. In the past, he would have argued that it would cost too much. This time, he willingly consented to spend the extra money and thanked me over and over again for agreeing to go.*

*We spent the first day of our counseling intensive in separate group sessions. The wives were encouraged to join phone support groups when we returned home. After the session, I asked the leader if there was a support group for women whose husbands were fantasizing about young girls. She didn't know of one, but I could join any support group. But I already had a support group that wasn't much support. I could not find a single person willing to say out loud their husband was sexually attracted to young girls. In my mind, I wondered how many other wives were holding a devastating secret, feeling alone just like me?*

---

"Sexual deviancy is different than a sexual addiction to pornography. Appropriate treatment should be sought from an experienced clinical psychologist." Dr. Mary Dietzen

---

*The intensive turned out to be extremely intense for me. In our joint session, I heard again Jacob's confessions to the counselor of how deviant his fantasies had spiraled. He also confessed he wanted to act on them. I was sitting there living a nightmare. While still shocked at his admission, I managed to hear the counselor say they could administer a lie detector test to Jacob to make sure he hadn't already acted on his fantasies. The counselor asked if I wanted Jacob to take one. I managed to blurt out, "Yes!" What I wanted more in that moment was for someone to administer something to me. I wanted a sleeping pill so strong it would take away the pain and I would never wake up.*

*As soon as I could stand without falling over, I left the room, headed for the bathroom and threw up. I sobbed and cried out to God for strength. I shook as the fear of what might be true strangled me. The thirty-five minutes of waiting for the results of the lie detector test felt like an eternity. I wanted to run, head straight to the airport and catch the next flight home. But it dawned on me that Jacob had our tickets in his coat pocket. I could do nothing but wait. Finally, the counselor called me into his office. Jacob was sitting there. He had passed the polygraph. The fantasies had not become real life. The good results of the test did nothing to relieve the pain. His confession still felt like a giant knife stabbing my heart.*

"There is a reason why polygraph results aren't admissible in court: they don't prove guilt or innocence. Research shows that a high percentage of deviant offenders can pass a polygraph because they believe their own lies, rationalize, or minimize the offense." Dr. Mary Dietzen

*The counselor gave Jacob the name and number of a guy where we lived who successfully overcame his fantasy life. We made a plan. He was never to be around the grandkids again. Jacob would quit his custodial job. No more being around girls of any age. He was to join a second sexual addiction group and contact the guy they recommended for accountability.*

*We left the office and headed to the airport in silence. While at the gate waiting to board, Jacob apologized and cried. He promised to work hard and beat "this." Jacob could not name his sin. He kept saying how grateful he was that I would stick by him. I was his strength and the reason*

*he would be more determined to overcome "this." The sharp pain turned to feeling numb. If it hadn't dulled, I doubt I would have survived it.*

# Lynn

## Behind Closed Doors—The Last Straw

*During our separation, one of the things that made a big impact on Paul and increased his affection for me was a Valentine's Day gift I gave him. He loved horses and had always revered Jacob Lyons. I discovered this well-known trainer was offering classes at his ranch in Colorado and purchased a week's training for Paul to enjoy that summer. I wrapped a large picture book about Jacob Lyons with a certificate for the training inside the cover. Paul was overwhelmed when he opened it, citing how amazed he was by my love and thoughtfulness.*

*But this awe of me faded almost immediately. The cycle of abuse continued. Worse yet, his dissatisfaction with me was becoming more frequent resulting in shorter reconciliation and calm phases. In fact, by the time the scheduled trip together to Colorado approached, he made excuses and refused to attend. I was terribly hurt, sensing this was an ominous sign about our relationship. However, I decided not to cancel my scheduled vacation time, and made plans to do some things I enjoyed.*

*The first day of my vacation, I opened my laptop and his Facebook page appeared. The day prior, Paul, showing friends some funny videos posted from his class reunion, had left it open. I looked closely at his postings and noticed some private conversations that had taken place months prior, during our separation. My heart and stomach sank as I realized he was exchanging sexual videos with a woman during the time he was supposedly working hard on restoring our relationship. Angered, I called and confronted him, and he was furious at me for bothering him at work. My friend Glenda, who arrived to take me on a bike ride, found me sobbing on the floor of my closet.*

*I left that day, not at all sure of what I would do, but aware I couldn't stay at home. I checked into a local hotel to take time to gain some clarity.*

Sitting by the pool with a book, drinking Margaritas, I let anger take over. How could he betray me like this? The pain was so intense I didn't want to feel. I took off my wedding ring, put it in my pocket and kept on downing drinks. Eventually, I stumbled my way to the hotel room, fell into bed, and slept like a rock.

When I woke up, the anger had dissipated, and I had second thoughts about ending it. I reached in my pocket to replace my wedding ring, and it was gone. Desperate to find it, I tore the hotel room apart, and retraced my stumbling steps back to the pool, with no success. The symbol of my commitment was forever lost, and I felt guilty and distraught for allowing it to happen.

My friends were my lifeline. Jillian came by to lift my spirits and pray for me. She was not deterred by her own trial of slow recovery from back surgery. Even being unable to drive didn't stop her. She had Jacob drop her off, not just once, but every day that I stayed at the hotel. I spent long hours with Laurel on the phone, processing my feelings and discussing what I should do next. Laurel kept repeating, "This is no way to live." I felt anxious and so hurt that I couldn't think clearly. I wanted the pain to stop but hesitated to pull the plug on our twenty-seven-year marriage. Neither Laurel nor Jillian told me what to do; instead, they reminded me of what I had learned and asked me what I thought God was saying.

After a few days of me staying away, Paul agreed to keep a joint counseling appointment we had made a few weeks prior. I felt strong and honest as I spoke about my inability to tolerate any more betrayals. Paul got the message; he said, "You're telling me I have to choose." I felt heard and invited him to the hotel to talk further. Over dinner, the small movement he made towards me after counseling was withdrawn, and he pulled back. I responded by moving towards him to bridge the discomfort of the distance. The warmth returned, we felt drawn to each other, and he spent the night.

The next morning, energized by our romantic evening, Paul went home to pack a bag and returned. I felt hopeful and shared what I needed from him to rebuild trust. We rented bikes and laid by the pool, but I felt the distance *slowly return, and by evening Paul unleashed his anger about my "demands." I am ashamed to admit, I stood between him and the door to our hotel room, crying. I begged him to stay and talk it through. Instead of softening, he threatened to physically remove me from where I stood. A switch inside me flipped; I gathered my emotions and shut off my tears. I told him I wanted an opportunity to regain my dignity and let him go.*

*That was the last straw. I knew I could no longer continue to move towards him when he rejected me. This time, what kept me from allowing the pattern to repeat ad nauseum, was my concern for Laurel and Jillian. They had been with me through several trips around this same mountain; how could I keep trying with Paul and put them through that again? Initially, it wasn't concern for my own health, but concern for my friends, that helped me to be done. I decided to go home the next day and tell Paul he needed to move out.*

---

"In most cases, the abuser will not change, and the only way to end the abuse is for the victim to end the relationship." [51]

---

*A few days after I succeeded in getting Paul to pack up and leave, I received a call from his employer. He asked if I knew where Paul was, and if I was still married to him. I answered yes to both questions; he was in the Ukraine on business and we were separated but still married. Paul had told his work a different story; he was taking his sister to the Mayo Clinic for treatment of a rare genetic condition. His coworkers discovered that instead he went to the Ukraine. Additionally, they found evidence he had been sending money to women there. His boss shocked me by adding that Paul had embezzled more than $30,000 from his company. His advice: take immediate action to protect myself financially.*

*I took the call when driving on the freeway and pulled over to the shoulder, trying to absorb the shocking news. My brain couldn't seem to take it in. I knew Paul was capable of deceit, but embezzling? The next hours were a blur; I got back on the road to travel a well-known route and got lost three times on the way. Nothing looked familiar; I could not make sense of my new reality and had no idea where to turn next.*

*Over the next week, the way forward became clearer, one step at a time. I met with each of my kids to tell them in person what I had learned about their dad, and my plan to divorce. They asked very few questions and showed little emotion. I retained the services of an attorney, consulted with my pastor, and filed for divorce. I was now fully resolved that I did not need to work on my marriage any longer. I was done.*

## 9

# Transformed

Cinderella emerged from the locked room looking the same but **behaving differently.** She was **strong,** and **no longer feared** her past abuse that had been a barrier to the fulfillment of her **dream.** When the opportunity to try on the slipper presented itself, even the step mother's **gross misconduct** didn't deter her. She **bravely** and **confidently** identified herself as the girl whom the prince loved by presenting the other glass slipper. Her crystal-clear identity was confirmed when she tried on the slipper and it fit perfectly.

## 9.1 A New Step of Forgiveness

After several years cocooned and isolated from my parents, I thought God had released me from a relationship with my dad. I continued to miss my mom but had given up having a relationship with her while my dad was still alive. Despite my lack of contact with them I continued to work on forgiveness. But it was a process, not an event.

Don't get me wrong, I didn't like my dad. I hadn't forgotten what he did. What I chose to forgive or let go of was the debt. In my mind, what he had done to me was now between him and God. Did I wish he would admit it and say he was sorry? Sure! I still held out hope that one day he would. I also prayed he would get right with God and me before he died.

But about this time, my son Kenney challenged me to reengage in relationship with my dad. "Mom, you need to forgive him," he said. I thought Kenney knew of my efforts and was offended by his suggestion that I should be doing more about the relationship! I protested, "What do you mean, Kenney? I have forgiven; they don't want a relationship with me!" "When's the last time you tried mom?" he said. "I think you need to reach out to them."

Much to my surprise, as I prayed about it, I began to sense that God was indeed changing my marching orders. Although the time of separation had given me much needed space to get stronger, it wasn't meant to be permanent. I sensed God urging me to reach out to my parents despite any lack of repentance or remorse.

This was a BIG ASK! I was not at all happy about the idea. In fact, the proposition that I seek out my parents after the lengths they had gone to cover up the truth, seemed downright unfair. Did God really want me to hang out with the man that raped and abused me for years? And if so, why?

It would be a long time coming before I knew the answer to those questions. But eventually, I realized that being in relationship with my dad after a period of healing was GOOD FOR ME!

## 9.2 Calm and Confident

One night after Kenney's phone call, I had a very vivid dream that included my parents. In it, my mom was redoing her house, and there were two spare rooms. One was brand new. It was on the main floor, had lots of windows, and was very inviting. I went to see her, and after admiring the room, I hoped to stay there. But, instead, she led me downstairs to the basement where she had cleared a space for me to stay. I was disappointed; I wanted the new room. At the end of the dream, my mom said she wanted to give me some of her china.

Within a week, I received a phone call from my mom. We talked as if nothing was wrong and no distance existed between us. Her denial of the current situation was not unusual, but something else was. She kept pausing to ask my dad, "Is that right, Larry?" Obviously, my dad was right there. Eventually she handed him the phone.

Unlike in the past, I was unusually calm talking to him. He began by telling me they had joined a church and went on to describe the many philanthropic volunteer roles he now held in the community. I couldn't help but feel he was giving me a resume of his good works. However, he also shared that both he and my mom's health had declined. His MDA was advancing, and she had been diagnosed with Alzheimer's. "The doctors said that the stress you're putting her under is responsible for its rapid progression," he said.

"The stress I am putting her under?" I said. "Yes," he replied. And just as he started to make another dig, I said, "That's enough! I am not going to be talked to this way." To which he replied, "Well, I guess you've changed!"

I don't think he meant it to be, but I took this as a HUGE compliment. Changing the subject, he told me my mom wanted to invite me to attend a women's Christmas Program being held at their church. I accepted the invitation, welcoming the chance to see her.

The call ended with my mom and I planning to meet for the event. Before hanging up, she said "Oh, I've been doing some weeding out, and I have some china for you. Maybe we can drop it by sometime!"

Later, as I reflected on the dream I had had the week before, I felt sure the china was in no way a coincidence. The message of the dream seemed to be that my mom was making room in her life for me. It was not the room I wanted, not the authentic, new relationship I desired, but rather, it was going to look more like what I had experienced with her in the past.

After going so long without her in my life, I decided the old room was better than no room at all.

## 9.3 Empowered

I attended the Christmas event with my mom, and a few weeks later, called my folks and asked if we could stop by. Mike, the kids, and I planned to make a short, cordial visit on Christmas Eve. My mom enthusiastically agreed, offering to make dinner for all of us. I was in no way ready for that, and politely declined.

We arrived at their house when it was dark. There were Christmas lights hanging from the eaves, and I could see their small tree in the living room as my mom opened the front door. My heart was warmed by the mere sight of her and I gave her a hug. The four of us entered the house; a house I hadn't visited in over four years.

My dad stood up from his chair and walked sheepishly over to say hello. I purposefully looked him straight in the eye and returned the gesture. "Hi there." The whole experience was nothing like I imagined it. It was very easy for me to be warm and kind and interacting with dad was overall uneventful.

My mom went into the kitchen, and we conversed easily while she dished up some dessert for us. Meanwhile, Mike went into the living room with my dad. Mike noted later, that my dad was wiping tears from his eyes as the two of them sat down.

Eventually, Kelsey, Kenney and I made our way to the living room. With all of us together, we proceeded to have a superficial but cordial conversation. I remember looking at my dad in his frail condition and having difficulty seeing him as the same monster who had viciously raped and assaulted me all those years ago.

The visit lasted a total of thirty-five minutes and ended shortly after we finished our dessert. As we left, I felt strong. Facing the person who had caused me immeasurable pain and suffering, and doing it so unapologetically in love, was empowering.

## 9.4 Moving On

I walked into the new year with more time and emotional margin than I had had in years. I started doing some of the things I used to enjoy like working out, decorating, gardening, and painting. I love to paint. Walls, furniture, household items, you name it, I'll paint it. My mother-in-law used to say I'd paint Mike if he held still long enough!

My love to create found a whole new outlet when my daughter and her boyfriend Fred announced their engagement that Spring. They decided to get married in the church, but the reception would be held in our backyard. Although there was more than enough space, we would need to do quite a bit to get our yard "wedding-ready." Mike and I got busy installing a DIY water feature, pergola, firepit, and dance floor. Meanwhile, Kelsey and I started planning and preparing all the Pinterest ideas we could find.

I loved getting ready for their wedding; the only thing even remotely stressful was the guest list. Kelsey and Fred were unsure what to do about my folks. "Mom, do you want them to come?" they asked me one day.

Honestly, that was a loaded question. On one hand, if I was moving on and putting the past behind me, why shouldn't they come? I had told my dad we could agree to disagree on the past, and that I had let it go. He had also agreed to, in his words, "Bury the hatchet." The wedding could provide us both the opportunity to walk that out.

On the other hand, despite what had been said prior to the engagement, my dad was unpredictable at best. It felt risky to invite him to such an important event. Would he be able to be civil? Would he cause a scene? Also of concern: how would my dad's attendance affect my ability to enjoy the wedding?

Ultimately, I opted to let Kelsey and Fred make the decision whether to invite my parents. They chose to give them an invitation to the ceremony and reception but decided not to include them in the rehearsal dinner or photographs.

## 9.5 Enjoying Myself

My goal of not discussing the past seemed near impossible for my dad. Leading up the wedding, the few exchanges we had usually included the question, "If you think I did what you say, why would you want to have a relationship with me?" My answer was always the same. "Because I have forgiven you and am moving on." One time he asked me if I believed he raped me. Unsure how wise it was, I decided to answer him honestly, "Yes I do." It was strange, he didn't argue with me, it was as if he just wanted to know the extent of my recollections.

Consequently, I had real questions about what he would be like at the wedding. Had we made a mistake? A few weeks prior to the wedding, my parents came over to our house and after they left, I felt better about the decision to invite them to the wedding. During the visit, although my dad looked very uncomfortable, my mom was obviously glad to see us. She smiled sweetly, was warm, affectionate and complimentary. While Mike took my dad out to see the shop he had built, Kelsey and I engaged my mom in conversation in the living room.

My heart swelled as my Mom and I spent time together. We talked about the wedding plans, her garden, and cooking—her favorite topic of all. When she told Kelsey and me she didn't cook or bake anymore, "because things just weren't turning out," I didn't know what to think. My mom was a Home Economics major and had always been passionate about creating in the kitchen. It took a minute to figure out that her dementia was probably making it difficult to follow a recipe. Like my dad had warned, the disease was progressing.

When the day of the wedding arrived, I woke up determined to enjoy my daughter's big day, no matter what! The only thing I was slightly stressed out about was my dress. The ten pounds I planned to shed so that my dress fit comfortably had not fallen off as expected. Consequently, I worried that the zipper wasn't going to hold. But thankfully it did... that is until about ten minutes before the ceremony started. I was in the lobby of the church, with a shawl around my shoulders when I felt it give way. Running into the women's bathroom, I found a stall, slipped out of the dress, and managed to get the zipper back on track. That was stressful!!

Also stressful was the anticipation of seeing my parents. But as I walked back into the lobby, and saw my folks standing there, I felt… nothing. I didn't feel awkward, fearful, or sad. Like the visit at Christmas, and my house earlier that summer, it was easy to be warm to my mom. She greeted me by saying I looked different than expected. She actually said she didn't recognize me. Was it the extra weight I was carrying at the time? I didn't know, and honestly, I didn't care. It felt so good to be free of the anxiety I once had about what they thought of my appearance.

The ceremony was beautiful, touching and sweet. Fred is from Kenya, and there were elements of his culture and tradition in the service and at the reception that followed in our backyard. For instance, the Kenyan community of women provided dinner at the reception to over 200 guests! I have no idea what we ate that night, but it was delicious! And dance… oh how we danced! Fred and his family taught us some new moves, and we stomped, jumped, and twirled the night away! It was an absolute blast. I had the time of my life despite the fact my dad was obviously pouting and miserable the entire time.

At one point, I caught sight of my parents. Standing a good distance away, I could see my dad and mom sitting at one of the reception tables. His head bowed, he stared at his hands resting on the table in front of him while my mom appeared to dote on him. It was a familiar scene. They left without saying goodbye not long after dinner was served. For most of my life, my dad's behavior that night would have affected me emotionally. But, not anymore. I was slowly realizing what it was like to be free and I really LOVED IT!!

I did find out later, that my dad's disposition had been troubling to Kelsey during the service. Sitting front and center, my dad had his arms crossed the whole time and looked angry. Kelsey avoided looking his direction as a result. Because of this, when my son married two years later, my parents were not invited.

## 9.6 Consistent Misbehavior

After the wedding, I continued to offer relationship and assistance to both of my parents as their health continued to decline. However, each time I extended my hand to them, it was met with rejection. My dad and mom would verbally agree to call me, or accept my help, but then later change their mind and leave me hanging.

Over Thanksgiving that year, I did see my brother and his family. We met at Kelsey and Fred's house. Brett and I had continued our relationship, mostly over the phone. It was hard for both of us, but his diligence to pursue me despite the tension in our relationship spoke volumes.

During the conversation that night, I casually mentioned something about a recent exchange with my folks. Jasmine, Brett's wife, seemed surprised and said, "Wait, you mean you have called and talked to your parents?" I said, "Yeah, usually they don't respond, but I've called and offered to help out." Jasmine and Brett looked at each other, concerned. Sensing their discomfort, I made the comment, "I have forgiven dad, and am moving on. I've asked him to agree to disagree."

We learned that night my dad was telling the family quite a different story. He said I was the one refusing to speak to them, and that when we did talk, I couldn't stop talking about the past. Brett was upset with him; I was underwhelmed. This was disappointing, but not at all surprising. My dad's behavior was remaining quite consistent. I had been the scapegoat my whole life. Why would it stop now?

## 9.7 Confronting, Not Pretending

Months went by without any communication with my mom. One day, I was praying, and felt God might be saying to go see her. Nervous, I decided to call Jillian for help. She was gifted in praying and sharing what she heard in response. After she answered the phone, I asked her to pray for me. When she asked what the request was, I refused to tell

her anything specific so as not to influence her. She stopped what she was doing, and over the phone, began to ask God for His help. Then she paused, and said, "I feel like God is saying, 'do it for your mom.' Does that make any sense to you?"

I could hardly believe my ears; I got the confirmation I wanted! I called Kelsey, and she agreed to go with me. Two hours later, we were standing on my parents' doorstep ringing the doorbell.

My mom was the one to answer the door. She seemed happy to see me, we hugged, and I said, "Mom, you haven't returned any of my phone calls. I haven't known what to do." Her response, "Well of course you didn't. I'm so sorry. We were just talking about you last night and I told your dad we aren't handling this right."

That's all I needed to hear. She was sorry. As we walked into the living room, I noticed my dad talking on the phone in the next room. Kelsey, my mom, and I had a few minutes to visit before he joined us.

"It's good to see you," he said as he took a seat in the chair next to me. My reply without thinking was, "Really? I doubt that." My words surprised even myself. Had I planned to pick a fight? No!! What got into me I don't know. All I can say is that I was angry for being ignored then lied about, and I was done faking it.

It's no surprise my words ignited his anger. Raising his voice, he said, "You're not going to come out here and talk to me like that in my own home." I think my dad had a good point. I had come uninvited. My choice of words and tone were confrontative. "I'm upset dad. I call and leave messages and yet you don't call me back. I thought you were going to bury the hatchet," I said. The conversation digressed as he angrily stood up and yelled, defending his actions by citing my failures as a daughter.

My mom, who had been sitting next to me, scooted over, turned her head and started to talk to my daughter about what might as well have been the weather. Meanwhile, I stayed seated, and was neither emotional nor afraid. I just was tired. Tired of all the lies. Confronting it, rather than pretending, seemed more natural to me.

When my dad said something about how he and my mom loved me, it was my daughter who spoke up and said, "How would my mom know you loved her?" "What did you say?" he shot back. Kelsey rephrased her question: "Love is an action. What actions are there to support the words you love her?" To which my dad responded, "Well, aren't you smart!"

The argument ended with a commitment to once again, in his words, "bury the hatchet." Rather a disturbing image, if you ask me. And then, without skipping a beat, my dad did the oddest thing. He invited Kelsey and me to tour the house with him. Again, like in my childhood, he had blown off his steam at me, and then acted like nothing happened.

For the next hour, we followed him around room by room, as he showed us all their material possessions, emphasizing their history and or value. While I hadn't toured their home in years, I was well acquainted with their stuff. I couldn't understand what was going on until he stopped, and said, "I don't want any of our things taken to the Goodwill when it's time." Apparently when my mom's parents moved to an assisted living facility, her sisters donated some of their furniture and things to charity. This really bothered my dad. In that moment something became very clear. My dad was more concerned about the future of his possessions than the future of his relationship with me. Although not surprising, I left their home that night with little hope I would be able to have a relationship with my mom while he was still alive.

## 9.8 Compassion

The way my dad manipulated my mom's relationship with me gave me unique insight into Lynn's relationship with her children. I knew what it was like to be the daughter of a mom who was in an emotionally and verbally abusive marriage.

One time, after Beth, Lynn's middle child, returned home from college, I got an alarming phone call. It was late, and Lynn was in a crisis as a result of an argument between Paul and Beth. She described how when things had gotten out of hand, Paul threw a ketchup bottle at Beth, hitting her in the back.

I was both shocked and concerned. To my knowledge, Paul had never physically assaulted Lynn or the kids before. I encouraged her to report it to the police, and get Beth to a safe place, even offering to let her stay with us. She was reluctant, and I felt conflicted.

After some convincing, Lynn brought Beth to our house, but didn't file a police report. I deeply regret not reporting it myself. In honoring Lynn's request to keep what happened confidential, I kept the physical assault from Mike and the authorities.

Beth stayed with us for several weeks, and Lynn came by numerous times and tried to convince Beth to pursue reconciliation with her dad. But Beth seemed determined to take a stand against Paul's assault and was not willing to go back home. Instead, she wanted financial help to get her own place. I agreed with Beth but felt like I was walking a tight rope with my friend. I encouraged Lynn to seek advice from a counselor, while at the same time I tried not to guilt her into taking action.

It would be many years later, after the divorce, before Lynn confided in me the extent of the physical abuse she and the kids had suffered. At first, I found her confession personally painful. Although I knew the root of her secrecy was denial and shame, I had been her best friend, a best friend who held none of my pain and abuse back from her. When I shared my feelings with her, she explained that not protecting her children, was inexcusable in her mind.

I felt differently. I knew Lynn was a victim. And as a victim, she had been, in effect, brainwashed by Paul for years. It took completely severing the relationship with Paul, and counseling to undo the damage.

What I learned from Lynn while experiencing feelings of betrayal and hurt from my own mother's inability to stand up for me, was tremendously helpful. It gave me needed insight and compassion for my own mom during this desperate season in both our lives.

## 9.9 Courage

My dad's declining health eventually resulted in hospitalizations every few months. During these episodes I was often contacted by a family member and a request was made to help my mom. Her dementia, now advanced, made driving to the hospital to see my dad out of the question.

I welcomed these opportunities. While it was clear her personality and ability to communicate were changing, I still cherished any time I got to spend with her. The fact that we were alone, without my dad, was an added bonus. In between hospital visits, we often found time to sneak in a latte at a local coffee shop or visit a department store to do some shopping. These were activities my dad usually disapproved of.

However, on one of these visits I arrived and found her still in bed. My mom, an early riser, refused to get up even though it was nearing lunch time. As I put my hands on her shoulders, and tenderly asked her if she wanted to go see my dad, she rolled over and said, "No."

This was most unusual. I wondered if she was confused, depressed, or both. Eventually, I coaxed her out of bed, and she made her way to the living room. As she sat down, I learned it was my relationship with my dad that was on her mind. "I just don't know what to do about all this hostility," she said. Looking at her, I replied, "Mom, I don't have any hostility in my heart toward dad. I have forgiven him and am moving on. But he can't let it go, and there is nothing I can do about that."

I'll never forget what she said next nor how she said it. "Well, YOU have a lot of COURAGE!" I knew beyond a shadow of a doubt what my mom was saying to me. In a moment of lucidness, she admitted that I had courage to stand up to him, courage she lacked but wished she had.

My mom's betrayal had been very painful for me. Far more painful than my dad's. But I knew that she was a victim too. I often had to remind myself of this fact, and it helped me forgive.

## 9.10 Validated and Victorious

In the months that followed, I was invited in and out of my parents' life. If they could find no one else to help them, I was in. Otherwise, I was out.

One day, after another one of my dad's hospitalizations, my brother invited me to attend one of my dad's follow-up doctor appointments.

Seeing it as a sign of progress, I joined them. That day, I heard the doctor deliver the news that my dad's MDS had converted into leukemia. As the doctor laid out the plan of care and discussed the need for chemotherapy, my dad remained calm and composed.

As we left the office and got into the elevator, both Brett and I reassured my folks that we were willing to help in any way we could. An awkward silence ensued, and by the time we reached the lobby, my dad's emotions erupted. It was a familiar experience. Just like in the good ol' days of my past, instead of owning his anger, he unleashed it on me. As he turned to face me, I watched as he went from zero to 100 on the anger Richter Scale in just a matter of moments. His face got red, his eyes narrowed, and his body shook as he screamed, "I didn't do what you said I did!"

Really? Now? Here? I couldn't believe he was going to make a scene. However, unlike years past, his anger didn't make me cower or clam up. Instead, once again I felt strangely calm. With my mom and brother looking on, I firmly said, "Dad, I feel very badly about what you are about to go through, and I would like to help out, but I will not be talked to this way anymore."

For just a second, time seemed to stand still. I wasn't sure what his next move was going to be. Was he going to lash out at me? Would he continue to create a scene? I braced myself. But, to my surprise, he did neither. Instead, he stormed out of the lobby without saying a word.

Oddly enough, both Brett and my mom lingered behind. My brother said, "You didn't deserve that," and my mom gave me a hug as my dad looked on through the glass doors from where he stood in the parking lot. It was a risky move on their part, and I wondered what the cost of comforting me would be for them later. I reassured them both I would be fine, and they left. To have both my brother and mom validate me for speaking up and setting boundaries on my dad's behavior was a departure from the family pattern. As I watched them catch up with my dad, I felt encouraged, strong, healthy, and victorious.

### 9.11 Having Fun

After the leukemia diagnosis, my dad continued to resist relationship with me despite my efforts. I took meals and called to make myself available to him and my mom, yet my dad lied and complained to my brother that I refused to help. Instead of me, I learned that Dad asked Brett's friend from high school to take them to appointments or assist with groceries when needed. My dad's ongoing behavior felt like rejection, but I responded by letting go. I had done what I could and was not going to force my way into their lives.

Meanwhile, Mike and I were having the time of our lives being empty-nesters. We sold the eighteen-foot boat we had enjoyed during the years we raised our kids and purchased a thirty-foot cruiser that was moored in Priest Lake Idaho. Referred to as the "crown jewel" of Idaho, Priest Lake is surrounded by miles and miles of undeveloped mountains and forest. We loved being there and made the hour-and-a-half trip to stay on our floating cabin every weekend from March to October.

Consequently, I became a walking advertisement for owning a boat on Priest Lake. One day Lynn mentioned she was thinking of going back to school to get her master's degree. She had just come through her divorce with Paul, which of course was a very stressful and emotional time in her life. I hated the idea she would choose something so serious and difficult as her next step and told her so. "I think you should do something fun!" I said. "Like what?" she asked. Without any thought at all, I said, "Like get a boat!" Before I knew it, we were looking up ads for used boats and within the week made a trip to check one out.

"Kahlani's" owner had passed away, and her husband, also in poor health, was trying to sell her. Our hearts went out to him as he affectionately gave us a tour of all the boat's amenities. I thought it was perfect. It had a cuddy cabin for sleeping, and a full canvas, something I knew Lynn would need during the cold spring and early summer evenings at the lake.

Lynn purchased the boat, and soon, my friend was also coming to the lake every weekend. Mike loved it... I had a playmate, someone with whom I could hike, berry pick, fish, and kayak. This meant he could do what he loved: sit on the dock and entertain our dock neighbors with his numerous police stories. He always had a captive audience!

## 9.12 Subterfuge

Another benefit of the lake was seeing more of our longtime friends Lizzy and Brent. They lived near the marina and often had us over for dinner around their outdoor fire pit. During one of those dinners, I got a call from my Aunt Penny. She informed me my mom was in the hospital and needed support. I hesitated, not because I didn't care, but because my dad had clearly demonstrated I was not welcome in their lives. I told Penny I didn't think my dad would want my help.

"No," she said, "We've talked to him and he has agreed to it. Laurel, I made him promise not to bring up the past." "Ok," I said. "Of course." Within minutes of hanging up with Penny, my dad called. He reported after my mom had spent three days in bed unable to eat, drink or get up, he was advised to have her taken by ambulance to the hospital.

I was very concerned and asked my dad if I could visit my mom the next day. He agreed, and then without skipping a beat said, "Why don't you go get a polygraph test done?" It was so off topic, I had to clarify what he was talking about. "I didn't do what you are saying I did. You need to get a polygraph!" he said. The commitment he made to my aunt had lasted less than ten minutes. I responded as I had for months, "Dad, I am not going to talk about this with you anymore. We need to agree to disagree on what took place in the past."

As I hung up the phone, it was obvious my dad was not going to be able to "bury the hatchet." And yet, my mom clearly needed me. I went back to the campfire, where my friends and Mike were gathered, and shared my concerns.

Lizzy understood exactly the dilemma I was facing. Her mother had verbally and emotionally abused her and her sisters. At times, it was so bad, that Lizzy feared for her life. Her father, like my mother, had never been able to stand up to his wife, and consequently, suffered years of abuse himself. He, like my mom, now had dementia.

Thus, when Lizzy gave me advice, I listened because I knew it came from a place of experience. She looked at me from across the fire, and said, "Laurel, the only way to be involved, and help your mom, is for you to be an actress." "An actress?" I said. "Yes. Maybe by the time you are done you'll win an academy award!" she said. We all laughed, the humor providing a welcome reprieve.

"But Lizzy, I've spent years trying to get rid of this 'nice-girl' mentality with my folks, and am finally comfortable being authentic. Being an actress seems like going backwards and contrary to what I learned in counseling," I said.

Lizzy explained that my dad was not going to change. He was not responding to my authenticity; it just created an environment for further conflict. She insisted that if I wanted to help my mom, I was going to need to change strategies and become an "actress."

I went back to the boat that night, and the next morning woke with a word in my mind: *subterfuge*. Unfamiliar with its meaning, I looked it up. The English dictionary defines subterfuge as a strategy using "deceit in order to achieve one's goal."[52] I sensed God was confirming Lizzy's advice: being an actress with my dad was the strategy I needed to evade arguments and help my mom.

## 9.13 Suspicions

I went to visit my mom the next morning at the Skilled Care Unit of the retirement community where they now lived. She recognized me immediately, and then started to cry. "Where have you been? It's been so long since I've seen you," she said. My heart broke into a million pieces in that moment. I felt I had failed her yet wasn't sure what I could have done differently.

I sat with her for hours and observed the difficulty she had keeping her eyes open, even after waking from long periods of sleep. It appeared as if she was under the influence of drugs, but the staff said otherwise. It took several days, but she finally recovered and was released to go home. Clinically, there was never a diagnosis to explain her sudden downturn.

Later, both her case manager and I suspected my dad had given my mom Valium and or Xanax, in order to keep her sedated and home while he was gone for his all-day chemo treatments. I found both those drugs in their cottage. Allegedly, my dad didn't want to pay the money for a caretaker, despite the fact that my mom had a history of wandering and getting lost in his absence.

Therefore, the first chance I got, I removed all the sedatives from the house, along with the guns, and took them home with me. Why the guns? My dad kept mentioning to me he had hoped my mom and he would die together at the same time. My aunt had also shared a similar conversation she had with my parents the year before. It was an extreme notion, but not one that was out of the question.

## 9.14 Acting My Way to a Feeling

After my mom was released from the hospital, I continued my role as an actress in order to stay involved in her care. This meant faking affection and concern for my dad. In a tone and manner that was completely inauthentic, I said things like, "How are you today, Dad? You look tired, are you okay? What can I do for you?" Gag me. What I would have liked to say is, "You look tired Dad, maybe if you didn't spend so much energy and time trying to make me look bad, you'd feel better."

Obviously, my love and forgiveness for my dad wasn't anchored in warm, fuzzy emotions. Instead, I made the decision to show my dad love by caring for him despite my feelings. And I demonstrated forgiveness by choosing to let go of his past offenses despite his lack of remorse. And this was both DIFFICULT and COSTLY.

But much to my surprise, over time, I "acted" my way to genuine feelings for the man. What started as obedience, grew into something entirely different that looked and felt a lot like compassion.

For example, one day, I arrived at their cottage, and discovered my mom was having something that resembled a three-year-old's tantrum. While she cried, pouted, and threatened to leave, my dad rested his head on the kitchen counter and wept. "Dad, what's going on?" I asked. "I just can't do it anymore, we need to move into assisted living so we can have more help," he said. "But your mom doesn't want to."

I actually felt sorry for him. Taking care of my mom in the state she was in was very difficult. It hadn't taken me long to figure that out. It was emotionally and physically draining. Left on her own, she didn't eat, bathe or change her clothes. My dad, very sick and weak from his own illness, could not give her what she needed. My mom, who had always kept herself at 125 pounds was now down to 103! She was losing weight right along with my dad.

That day, my dad agreed to let me help him get a crew of caregivers lined up to help them until they could move into assisted living. I called Jillian and asked her to come over. Jillian had been working with the elderly for years, and I was confident she would be a wonderful companion for my mom. True to form, she dropped what she was doing and came that same day to start caring for my mom. Another childhood friend of my mom's also offered her services, and between the three of us, we were able to provide help seven days a week.

## 9.15 Beginning to Be Believed

Over the course of the next few weeks, my dad's condition rapidly declined. He was weak, experiencing bouts of hallucinations, and short of breath. With the help of my mom's youngest sister and her husband, who traveled from across the state to visit, we convinced him he needed immediate medical attention.

After a short stint in the ER, he was admitted. The next morning, obviously unhappy about his situation, he was overtly hostile toward me. Brett spoke up in my defense, and my dad responded by saying, "I know we are all just acting, playing our roles. None of this is real." I played dumb, disappointed he had seen right through my "acting." So, it wasn't an award-winning performance after all?

Meanwhile Brett said, "Dad, there is no subterfuge going on here." I couldn't believe my ears. Did I actually hear that right? Who uses the word *subterfuge*? Honestly, you can't make this stuff up!

Just then, the nurse entered the room, putting a halt to the escalating tension in the room. I made a quick exit to the waiting room and soon thereafter started to get a headache that by afternoon had worked its way into a full-blown migraine. I didn't feel well enough to go into my dad's room when the doctor arrived on his rounds. I chose to stay in the waiting room. When my uncle and brother emerged from my dad's room, they said Dad had gotten some very bad news. The doctor told him the chemotherapy treatment was being discontinued and there was nothing left they could do for him.

I wasn't surprised but wondered how dad had taken the news. Brett and my uncle said he handled it all quite well. My uncle and Brett returned to be with my dad, but my uncle quickly reappeared looking shook up. He walked over to me, and very emphatically said, "I've never seen your dad like this before. You're not going back in there; those days are over!"

This was not the only statement made to me by family about my dad's behavior. Another came in the form of a phone call from Aunt Penny. "Laurel, I wanted to ask you about a conversation your dad said he had with you last night." "Okay," I replied. "Did your dad tell you that you need to stop talking about the past and agree to disagree?"

I laughed out loud at the utter absurdity. I couldn't help it. "No, he didn't. That is what I said to him! He just won't stop bringing it up!" I said. What my aunt said next was music to my ears. "Laurel, we want you to know that we realize your dad has been lying." All I could think was... finally!

## 9.16 Disinherited?

My dad was admitted to hospice, and eventually placed in the Skilled-Care unit on the campus where they lived. We moved my mom into an assisted-care room one floor away. Meanwhile, I started to get their cottage ready to sell. All this, while continuing to work. I was emotionally, physically and mentally exhausted. And what happened next didn't help.

One day, while I was packing up their belongings at the cottage, I came across some legal paperwork that had my name on it. I had learned from family members that my dad had repeatedly discussed removing me from my parents' will, but they had discouraged him from doing so. As I began to read through the document, I noted that every time my name was mentioned, there was a line through it and my Aunt Penny's name was written above it.

I can't say I was surprised; history was continuing to repeat itself. My dad's mom had done the same thing to him on numerous occasions. While standing in the living room, holding the document in my hand, my brother arrived at the front door. He had made the trip from across the state to see my folks and help me pack. I answered the door and handed him the addendum to the will. "Dad doesn't want me in the will," I said.

Brett, obviously aware the paperwork existed, said, "Yeah, so what? He never mailed it. Besides, don't you think I would have shared it with you anyhow?" I was speechless. This was a large sum of money we were talking about, and Brett could have easily used the fractured relationship with my dad to his advantage. The fact he didn't, spoke loudly to me. I said, "We could take it over to him and see if he wants to mail it," I said. Brett shook his head no, and the two of us never discussed it again.

Despite Brett's response, I carried the addendum in my purse for several weeks, unsure what to do. Did I really want my dad's money under these circumstances? I wasn't sure. I also gave some consideration to what my mom's wishes would have been had she not had Alzheimer's. After all, it was her money too. I believed she would have wanted Brett and me to share it. And finally, I remembered a comment my dad made to me during his recent hospitalization. He said, "If you were to go down to Charles Schwab right now, you'd find you're going to be one rich lady after I'm gone." Although I didn't have any idea what he was talking about at the time, I realize my dad's comment revealed he was fully aware I was still in his will. Eventually, I threw the paperwork away.

## 9.17 A Clear Conscience

The cottage was almost ready to be put on the market. Boxes of my parents' belongings were stacked in the garage, and all that remained was cleaning. As I ran the vacuum over the living room floor, I recalled a recent conversation that took place there about my dad's final wishes. When asked where he wanted to die, he had said, "Right here." "You want to die at home?" I clarified. "Yes," he had said. My conscience was stricken. I recalled the care I gave my sister when she passed away and felt I should be willing to do the same for my dad.

Not giving myself too much time to change my mind, I left what I was doing to go visit him. When I got to his room, God gave me an unusual amount of grace. I looked at my dad and became very sad. Tears stung my eyes and he said, "What's wrong?" "I have something serious to talk to you about," I said. This was dangerous territory I was about to enter, and I knew it. The news of what I had to say would be a shock, despite the fact the doctor had been very forthright about my dad's prognosis.

"What is it?" he asked. "Dad, you are dying. You might only live another week or two." I said. He paused, looked down, and then asked me, "Does your mom know?" "Yes," I said, "she knows."

I then gave him the option to die at home. He looked out the window and around the very sterile feeling room we were in at the time, and said, "This seems fine to me." Relief washed over me, and I said, "OK, well that's fine. I won't bring it up again unless you do."

That night, my dad refused to get into his bed although he was obviously very tired. When I asked why, he said, "I might not wake up." Clearly, he was no longer in denial. I put on my pastor hat and said, "If you don't wake up here, what do you believe will happen to you?" "I'll be in heaven," he said. "Yes, you'll be with Jesus, and Debbie, and your dad," I said. Yet, my words didn't seem to bring him any comfort.

The next day, I learned from the staff he was up all night long. When I took my mom to see him, his emotional temperature had changed, and he was openly irritated and angry. Convinced his hostile demeanor was a sign of delusion, my mom, while affectionately stroking my dad's head said to me, "He's not really here anymore." "Mom, he is too," I said. "No, he's not!" she insisted. "He's out of it." The irony was not lost on me, clearly, she was the one that was out of it! Then, as if to orient him, she grabbed a framed photo of my sister and me as toddlers and stuck it in front of his face. "Who's this?" she asked.

My dad, still obsessed with my false confession of abuse, was forced to look at a photo of Debbie and me at the age the sexual abuse started. His agitation escalated, and not long after that we left.

Every visit thereafter, my mom gravitated to that picture and my dad responded accordingly. Even after I removed the photo, my dad continued to be hard on my mom, clearly lacking any concern for her well-being. Consequently, one night, after my mom got up to use the restroom, I decided to intervene. Leaning over his bed, I said, "Dad, Mom and I are concerned about you, and we want to be here for you. But if you don't want that, if you want to be alone, then just say so."

I'll never forget the look that came over his face. He narrowed his eyes, pursed his lips, and hissed, "I DID NOT DO IT." He was still obsessed I had not changed my story! Before my mom returned, I said, "Ok, Dad, we'll leave you alone if that is what you want. When Mom gets back, I want you to say goodbye to her nicely, and we'll go." He did, and once outside the room, my mom cried out, "How can you say there is a God who loves us when 'this' happens?" I reassured mom that Jesus was weeping right along with her. But, to be honest, I was so tired of it all. Both my parents were upset, angry and yelling at me! I left that night wondering how much longer I could hold up.

## 9.18 Shell Shocked

The next day, Mike took a day off work to be with my mom so I could finish writing a series of teachings for a women's retreat scheduled for that next weekend. I had made the commitment months earlier and saw no way out of it. Before I began my work, I prayed, and two phrases came to mind: "Shell shocked" and "Paper-thin emotions." I mentioned them to Lynn later that night, when we met up for dinner. "What do you think it means," she asked. "I'm not sure, maybe I'm going to be shocked by something? Or maybe my emotions are paper thin," I said. We both agreed it didn't seem to fit and put the concern aside to work on the retreat teachings.

*Lynn's Reflections...*

*I got in my car to go home after meeting Laurel and my phone rang. It was Mike. The first words out of his mouth were, "Lynn, I'm shell shocked." That got my attention! Immediately my mind went to the discussion about what Laurel heard in prayer that day. As Mike described what he witnessed, I felt shocked myself.*

*Mike wanted my advice, wondering if he should tell Laurel. She was struggling as it was, and he wanted to protect her. We both agreed that adding further stress and sorrow before the retreat was not in her best interest. This news could wait. I went to the retreat with Laurel and kept the secret I knew would devastate my friend.*

## 9.19 Disappointed

Friday rolled around, and I felt ill-prepared for the retreat. My content was only loosely developed, and I was anxious as a result. I threw some clothes in a suitcase and was about to leave when I decided to go check on my dad. Against all odds, I was convinced that my story would end in God's glory. This was a promise I believed God had given me years earlier. It originally surfaced while studying for a Sunday message and then resurfaced frequently in prayer.

Every time I thought about what God's glory would look like in my story, the vision of a surprise ending played like a scene out of a good lifetime network movie. My dad would tearfully admit what he had done to my sister and me. In response, I would reassure him, "Dad there is still time to get right with God." My dad would pray and accept Jesus as his Savior. As a result, my family would finally know who to believe, I would be vindicated, and God? God's power, goodness, and mercy would be credited with saving my family. Unlikely? Yes, but I knew other victims who had witnessed a death-bed confession like this and believed it was possible.

However, when I got to the door of his room, it was obvious that God's glory wasn't going to be fulfilled that day—at least not in the way I had hoped. My dad, wearing only a t-shirt and adult diaper was sitting in a wheelchair near the door. "Hi, Dad," I said. He looked away, angrily grabbed the arms of the chair, and attempted to stand, completely ignoring me. A male caregiver was in the room and filled in the awkward silence for him. "Larry had a rough night," he said. "Oh," I said, as I watched my dad, who resembling a walking skeleton, stiffly strut into the bathroom. "Yeah," the caregiver said, "He's pretty uncomfortable."

After my dad was safely out of hearing range, the caregiver leaned closer and told me my dad was his only patient. "He punched the night nurse in the stomach when she was trying to give him a suppository last night." Embarrassed for him, I apologized, but the caregiver said, "That's okay, we'll get Larry through this."

I left his room, disappointed, but holding onto hope that the next time I saw him, there would be an obvious change of heart.

## 9.20 Damning Words

The retreat ended Saturday afternoon, and when I arrived home, our son Kenney was there. He had flown home from California for the weekend to support me.

Exhausted from speaking and ministering to the women at the retreat, I decided to go out for dinner with my family and postpone visiting my dad till the following day. Brett and his family joined us after checking in on my dad. They reported that he was sleeping soundly.

The next morning, I woke to Kenney's voice, "He's gone. Your dad died last night." I sat up in bed, processing the news. I didn't cry, I didn't feel sad. I didn't feel anything, except perhaps, relief.

Kenney and Brett left for home later that day, and the next day, I was left alone with only one thing on my mind. My dad's lack of remorse. There had been no confession or repentance. My story ended the way it started, with a mean-spirited dad who was incapable of loving me. Not only that, I had not been vindicated. There would always be a question in people's mind about my story of sexual abuse.

I thought about it all day and by the time Mike got home, I was quite upset. Mike looked at me concerned and said, "I hope you won't be mad at me." "What do you mean, why would I be mad *at you?*" I asked.

He walked over to the drawer where he kept his iPad and sat down next to me on the living room couch. "Lynn and I decided to wait to tell you this until after the retreat." Opening a document on his iPad, Mike started to read something that sounded like a police report.

*Mike's Report, 10-06-2014:*

*I showed up after work. Bev wanted to go see Larry but was having problems remembering how to get from the cottage to his room. We walked over and immediately Larry began yelling at her about not coming sooner. It was upsetting to her. After we left, she was crying, so we went to dinner at Buffalo Wild Wings. The two waitresses saw Bev was upset and did their best to comfort her. She responded, and started to smile, laugh and eat onion rings, which I found she loves.*

*10-07-2014 1100 hours:*

*I accompanied Bev Smith, Laurel's mom, during the day, and as we approached Larry Smith's room, saw him with a female pastor from the Presbyterian Church they attended. He was down to wearing a diaper, and we prayed for him. I still can't believe I did that. I was almost feeling sorry for the man.*

*Bev and I went and ran some errands. We went to lunch and Bev had more onion rings. I asked if she wanted to go see Larry and she said, "No, maybe later."*

*1612 hrs. second floor nurses' station:*

*Bev is ready to go back and see Larry. We walked in from the east side to the second floor where the skilled nursing part of the facility was. As soon as we walked through the door, I could hear yelling. I immediately knew it was Larry. We started down the hall and I saw Larry standing near the nurses' station and he was not alone. There were three or four other guys there, and several staff. Larry was yelling and didn't even notice us walking up. He was very angry. Larry yelled, "Yeah, I did it, so what if it happened? It was a long time ago, what does it matter now?"*

*Bev asked Larry to calm down. He wouldn't, instead, he continued to yell the same phrase all over again, "Yeah, I did it, so what if it happened... it was a long time ago, what does it matter now?"*

My dear husband finished, and putting his arms around me said, "I'm so sorry. I was so mad he actually admitted to it! I wanted to beat him to death right then and was mad as hell that I couldn't. I imagined the headline, 'Detective beats helpless man to death.' Then I left with your mom as fast as I could."

Sobbing, I was nothing but grateful. Now I would have no lingering fear or doubt... I had not "blown up my family" with contrived memories of abuse. The words "paper-thin emotions," and "shell shocked" given to me in prayer the morning Mike and my mom heard my dad's damning words, confirmed his guilt. Although I felt this confession would never hold up in the court of public or family opinion, it was enough for me. God had seen to it that I could move forward with my life in peace. I had given my dad every opportunity to do the right thing, and he chose otherwise.

## 9.21 Finishing Strong

I decided not to tell my brother about my dad's hallway confession. After all, my goal had never been to destroy his relationship with my dad. I also didn't know if he would accept it as truth. But living with that decision was difficult. Brett wanted my help planning the funeral. For several weeks I actively made arrangements to honor the life of the man who chose betrayal over reconciliation. It was the last thing I felt like doing. I let Brett take the lead, my aunt Penny helped, and I sucked it up and did my part.

Mike and my kids saw my struggle and repeatedly reminded me that I didn't have to go. I knew they were right, and yet I wanted to "finish strong." In honoring my dad, despite what he had done, I believed I was honoring God.

It was a costly decision, but one I don't regret. I endured the "cool reception" by many the day of the service. It wasn't hard to determine who had been deceived by my dad's version of history. But I was pleasantly surprised that there were many others who were nothing but warm and welcoming.

Lynn and Jillian were extremely supportive. They greeted and helped serve punch prior to the service. Other friends, like Lizzy and Brent, also attended the service for the sole purpose of supporting me. I derived strength from their presence as I sat through the video, eulogy, words of affirmation and my brother's glowing tribute to my dad. When it was over, I got up, walked down the aisle, and once inside my car, cried tears of relief. It was finally over.

## 9.22 Judging My Story

In the months following my dad's funeral, I struggled to come to terms with the way things ended. It didn't seem like the promise that my story would end in God's glory had come true. One morning while praying, the Scripture text, "My glory is revealed in suffering," came to mind. As I pondered that, it occurred to me that Jesus suffered and died to save the entire world. That means he paid the price, for every single person past, present and future. Some of these loved him back, but most did not. Most of those Jesus died to save were in fact His enemies at the time.

Now that's love! That's unusual and extravagant and revealed God's goodness and mercy. Which led me to my "Ah-ha moment." Was it possible, could it be true, that loving my dad, despite the fact he didn't love me back, revealed the glory of God in me to others?

I thought about the card I received from a family member. It said, "When you loved and cared for two people who obviously didn't deserve it, I saw Jesus in you." God's promise was fulfilled, just not in the way I had expected.

My mom survived my dad by two-and-half years. Her dementia continued to advance, and she was moved to my daughter and son-in-law's Adult Family Home. The memory care unit at the retirement center was full. The decision and move were difficult for my brother, who had promised my dad before he died that I would not be allowed to care for my mom. Even in death, he tried to keep us apart.

For years, I held out hope my mom and I would be able to reconcile and work through our past without my dad's interference. But clearly, her dementia was too advanced for that. It was a bitter pill to swallow and on my worst days, I rehearsed a list of losses that looked something like this:

- I lost my innocence at the age of two and experienced ongoing sexual abuse by my dad into my teen years.
- I lost my dear sister Debbie when I was only thirty-five.
- I lost years of relationship with my brother, mother and dad when I chose to get help.
- I lost my reputation when my dad chose to cover up the past by lying about me.
- I lost relationships with other family members when they didn't know what to do or how to help me.
- I lost a dad who caused me immeasurable pain and was never sorry for it, and now I'm in the process of losing my mom, who has end-stage Alzheimer's.

I knew I was "stuck," and returned to counseling with Janis for a short time to process my disappointment and grief. She helped me realize it was entirely possible that my mother's Alzheimer's and "forgetting" was God's way of paving the way for our time together after my dad's death. She adeptly pointed out, that history is the best predictor of the future. It was highly likely that even in my mom's right mind, at age seventy-six, she would have chosen denial over facing the truth of the past.

I hadn't considered this and was able to let go of my previous expectations and make the best of the time we had left. My mom had a rather large amount of money in her bank account, money we spent in ways my dad had always discouraged. We made weekly appointments for her nails and hair to be done, whether they needed it or not! She loved lattes, so every outing included a stop at Starbucks. And we shopped at stores like Nordstrom for things she "needed," completely undeterred by price tags.

We also enjoyed activities together like walking, gardening, and on Halloween, handed out candy to children. She always lit up when around children. We even made my daughter a baby quilt. I cut out, assembled, and positioned the squares on the machine, and then stood over her guiding the fabric as she sat in the chair and ran the presser foot. It was a little stressful on my end, but the smile on her face made it all worth it.

## 9.23 Intervention

Jillian continued to be my mom's paid companion several days a week after my dad died. She was so good with her, and mom thought they were lifelong best friends.

Meanwhile, my relationship with Jillian became increasingly complicated. Originally, when she first became aware of Jacob's sexual attraction to her grandchildren, she developed and maintained boundaries on his behavior. They separated multiple times as a result.

But, one day on the phone, she shared her plans to take one of her granddaughters on a trip. Jacob was going to drive, and she had booked a nice hotel. "Wait," I said. "You mean Jacob's going with you both?" "Yes," she replied. "We've had such a long, hard road, it's time to make some good memories together."

I got off the phone and the more I thought about it the more concerned I became. After discussing the situation with Lynn, we decided to address the trip with her in person at our weekly get together.

Jillian now refers to what took place that day as an *intervention*. In many ways, I guess it was. We all got our drinks and took a seat around a table in the corner. I was the first to launch into the issue at hand, telling Jillian how concerned I was she was allowing Jacob to be around her granddaughter. She seemed bewildered. "What do you mean?" she asked. "What do I mean? I mean that after all that's happened, it's just not right!" Again, Jillian seemed confused.

By this time, I was getting upset and blurted out, "Jillian, if you take him on that trip, then I will no longer be able to maintain this level of friendship with you. In fact, I will call your daughter and tell her about Jacob!"

Lynn rescued the escalating situation. "Jillian, you have done a good job maintaining the boundary of not allowing Jacob around your grandchildren. What's changed?" she asked.

Jillian asked, "Why wouldn't Jacob be around the kids?" I interjected, "Jillian, he had an ERECTION the last time they were all in the same room with him!"

"HE DID?" Jillian said. "I don't remember that. When did this happen?" Jillian's face went pale. Lynn and I exchanged glances of unbelief; it was clear she had blocked the whole thing.

Over the next hour, Jillian asked questions about Jacob's past, and we answered them. She became emotionally distraught, as if learning it for the first time. It was an awful experience for all of us.

Ultimately, Jacob didn't go on the trip, and Jillian was thankful for the "intervention." So, was I. It had never occurred to me that my mom could have blocked any memory or signs of my abuse. Jillian's experience made it clear that was entirely possible, maybe even likely, and helped my efforts to forgive my mom.

## 9.24 A Painful Goodbye

My mom's Alzheimer's advanced at a slow, steady pace, but accelerated near the two-year anniversary of my dad's death. She was admitted to hospice, and Lynn, now in a management role there, hand-picked her nurse.

The next six months, I encouraged my brother and other family members to visit and say their final farewells. She was well-loved, and everyone responded.

Emotionally exhausted by what felt like a very long goodbye, it was important for me to be with my mom when she died. I sat vigilantly by her bed, refusing to go home just as I had done for Debbie. Brett made the trip across the state, and less than six hours after his arrival, Lynn arrived. All of us congregated in the room and waited. Jillian joined us and sat on the edge of my mom's bed. She held both of her hands in hers, and began stroking them gently, giving her permission to pass. She responded and took her last breath. All of us began crying, and exchanged hugs, relieved her suffering was finally over.

Brett and I planned her memorial service together, and it was well-attended. My son, a pastor, officiated, and numerous family members shared fond memories of my mom during the service. I wasn't sure until the moment presented itself whether I would be able to talk publicly about my relationship with my mom. But I felt strong and shared the Mother's Day Tribute I had written years earlier. I wanted everyone there to know that despite everything that had transpired, I loved my mom.

# Lynn
## Behind Closed Doors—Waking Up to Reality

*When our marriage finally ended, at first there was a sense of relief and a time of peace. But gradually, I realized that some things inside me were still broken. I became aware that I was still numb to my feelings, still reluctant to disagree, and still had weak boundaries with men. The person who had caused me harm was gone, yet I still struggled. The divorce didn't solve that.*

*I began to wonder if I would ever be whole. Was it possible to unlearn the unhealthy patterns developed over such a long time? The answer was yes, but it took a lot of work. I had already worked so hard on changing myself during the marriage, but I wasn't done. Like Laurel, I needed to be* out of the relationship with the one who abused me and completely disconnected from the cycle of abuse in order to see myself clearly. After Paul was gone, I made the most progress. This is when the memories of abuse, which I minimized while in the relationship, came to my full awareness.

The way I coped while in the marriage was to avoid reality. Like the three monkeys, I chose to hear no evil, see no evil, and speak no evil. To become well I had to unlearn this pattern. But shame was a huge barrier. I felt ashamed in the beginning just for being divorced. I never thought it would happen to me. The first week I attended a support group at church, one of the staff pastors greeted me and asked, "Are you here for Women's Bible study?" My heart fell as I admitted, "No, Divorce Care." I didn't want to be a part of that group!

But joining that class was a simple step in the right direction. I needed to face reality and correctly identify myself in order to get the help I needed. Healing occurred when I learned to do the opposite of the three monkeys – hear the truth, see the truth, and speak the truth.

First, I had to hear the truth about my value. Even though my husband had rejected me, God still loved me deeply. I heard that truth repeatedly as I listened to Christian music during sleepless nights. I leaned on my friends to speak truth as well. I often processed my feelings over the phone with Laurel and Jillian and heard words of understanding and acceptance. I could trust the truth I heard from others when I didn't trust my own feelings.

Hearing the truth was the first and most important step in my healing. Until I believed I was worthy of love and respect, I couldn't face the truth about the damage done in my marriage. I was surprised when a friend invited me to attend an Abuse Recovery class. I didn't yet see that my marriage was abusive. I was so reluctant to belong to that group, that I asked the leader to meet with me one-on-one. Each week as we sat at her kitchen table reading the lessons, I grew in my understanding. The more I learned about abuse, the more clearly I could see that I had been a victim.

My wise counselor told me to ask God to bring to mind the memories of hurt and write them out. He coached me to write down three things:

*what happened, how it made me feel, and what it taught me about myself. I resisted this idea for some time; I knew it would be painful and I didn't want to relive those moments. But I also didn't want to stay broken, so I reluctantly let the memories resurface. When I processed them over time, I was able to identify several lies that I believed as a result: "I am unwanted, unloved. I have no voice, no impact. I am not worth protecting."*

*As I saw the truth about my experience and these lies, I revisited the truth about my value. Three facts I continually revisited were: "I am loved by God and others, my words and choices do matter, and I have not been destroyed." These are solid truths that I still hold on to. In order to remember them, I wrote each truth on a rock, and placed them in a glass jar that I keep in my bedroom. When I doubt my value or am discouraged about my circumstances, I can pick up a rock and hear the truth.*

*Getting honest about my marriage and my home life was (and continues to be) a slow process. Even after I acknowledged the abuse, I insisted to my friends that it wasn't that bad. In my mind, it was only the last five years of our marriage that were really difficult. But reading through my journals told a different story. Even the "good times" were not as rosy as I remembered. I neglected to mention or even recall the worst memories of physical violence. Allowing my husband to physically harm me, and not taking action, was shameful. I kept pictures of my bruises from the last assault, as protection, but only shared them with my divorce attorney.*

*Much more difficult than facing the truth about my marriage was looking at the part I played. I was not the only victim; my kids were victims too, and I had failed to protect them. Our home was not a safe place in which to grow up. I recalled a painful family counseling session, hearing from our kids about how Paul's anger affected them. Paul was told by the counselor, "Your kids are afraid of you. You think about the space and time between your rages; they worry every day that it might happen. It's different being on the tip of the spear than holding it at someone."*

*As I listened to Laurel share the pain of her mom's betrayal, I realized I made similar mistakes. I didn't want to be like her mother, and I could see how my kids felt through listening to her experience. I felt ashamed for not* being a strong "mother bear" for my children, for being afraid to speak up, for being powerless to make an impact. I recognized the bravery it took for Beth to refuse to return home after Paul's assault with the ketchup bottle. I wished I had been brave so she would not have needed to be.

When we divorced, my kids were seventeen, twenty, and twenty-three. Only the youngest lived at home. Paul quickly moved out of state and was busy with his new life. I was left to do the hard work of downsizing, selling our home, and moving. I found I wasn't the only one who felt suppressed anger bubbling to the surface. My kids were angry too, and I was surprised when it was directed towards me. I slowly grew to accept that their anger wasn't completely misplaced. I needed to own my part. My inaction, had at times, resulted in their harm.

I wrote a letter to each of my children, affirming their unique strengths, and voicing my regrets. In order to undo the pattern I had learned as a victim to "speak no evil," I now had to speak the truth. I asked them to forgive me.

I lost my voice in my marriage. Even when I tried to speak up, I was silenced. Part of learning to speak the truth was using the correct words. I freely admitted that Paul's explosive anger destroyed our family, but I still had trouble using the label "abusive." I had been choked, and even had pictures of the bruises, but I still didn't find the word fitting.

I was challenged to change this when asked to share my story with a group of women. As I prepared, I felt completely disconnected from it, non-emotional. I couldn't seem to get the words down on paper and didn't know what I was going to say. This didn't change until Laurel and Jillian encouraged me to use the correct words: abuse, anger, damage in our home. Once I did, a new level of freedom followed, and my emotions returned.

Speaking the truth about what was done to me and what I did to cope has been so painful, that if I hadn't heard the truth first of my worth, I would not be able to bear it. But I know I am loved and forgiven, and that helps me speak the truth about my shame, my pain, and my experience.

Because of this process, I am experiencing better relationships with my adult children. My girls are starting to speak to me more honestly, and *they come to me when they need a safe place. I partnered with my son instead of rescuing him, and he is successfully living independently.*

*I have a great job as a hospice nurse that I love. I am speaking up at work about things that need to change and am valued by my boss for doing so. I am more aware of my feelings and am no longer numb. Laurel and Jillian say I am more assertive and confident. Sometimes these changes are hard for me to see, but I trust them to tell me the truth!*

## Jillian

### Behind Closed Doors—Calling It What It Was

*After returning from Colorado, Jacob quit his custodial job and found a job doing office work. For the first time in twenty-four years, he worked at a forty-hour-a-week job. He added another sex addiction group, attending two per week, and contacted the recommended accountability partner. He was checking off all the boxes on the list. Jacob daily insisted he was doing great handling his addiction, talking about how relieved he was to be free of the fantasies. He wanted to come home. Both of us began to talk like "it" was behind us now.*

*Even though I wasn't completely open in my group, it did help in some ways. Through the exercises in the workbook, I got stronger at setting boundaries. With the help of my counselor, I wrote an agreement that Jacob and I both signed before he moved back in. It read like this:*

*I, Jacob agree to the following actions:*
- *I will attend my sex addiction class weekly.*
- *I will call my accountability partner daily to check in.*
- *I will call my accountability partner if or when I am tempted to fantasize instead of giving into the temptation.*
- *I will leave the lights on and talk with my wife during intimacy in order to stay connected and not fantasize.*

*My agreement was this:*

*I, Jillian agree to:*

- *Practice the communication exercises with Jacob from the workbook.*
- *Continue counseling.*
- *Hold firm to the specific consequences that we agreed upon. (These were also listed in the contract.)*

*It was good to write out my action plan. If Jacob lacked follow-through, we both knew in advance what would happen.*

*Jacob, instead of being free as I had hoped, continued to struggle with his addiction. He was aroused watching gymnastics on TV. When I found out, I implemented the consequences. He moved upstairs for a week, then he resumed following our agreement, so I let him move back downstairs with me. Later, he broke the contract again and I enforced a two-month separation. While away from home, he checked off the to-do list of every-thing I asked, so I allowed him to return. Why did I refuse to give up? I was afraid of failing. Three divorces at my age, meant I would probably spend the rest of my life alone. So, I stayed, believing a lie that it was my last chance to be loved.*

*The fear of being alone was intense. But staying was tearing me up in-side. I became hyper-vigilant, trying to keep him away from any interaction that might trigger his thoughts. I was fearful of him being attracted to girls we encountered at the mall or in the park, so we went out very seldom. I was afraid someone might capture his attention and rob us of what little we had left of our shaky relationship.*

*We kept the facade with family, friends and church that we had a hap-py marriage. This was difficult, especially with family. I would not allow Ja-cob in the same room with my grandkids. No more going to the beach to-gether, having them spend the night. My daughter and family had moved out of state. I began to make trips to see them alone and discouraged them from coming to visit us. When they came to town, he left the house and stayed elsewhere. They missed Jacob, but I continued to cover up why he was absent. I was ashamed of his secrets. The question, "How can I stay married to Jacob but keep those that matter most to me away from him?"*

consumed me.

What I didn't realize was how difficult it was to maintain the reality of Jacob's struggle while keeping it secret. Although I had faced the truth about my abortion and never forgot it again once it was recalled, I couldn't keep my eyes open to the truth about Jacob while I was in relationship with him. He referred to his sexual addiction as porn. In reality, Jacob had been aroused during very innocent interactions with girls. But I accepted his words and started calling it porn also. This rationalizing became our way of coping. After all, there's a lot of men addicted to porn, right?

Unfortunately, the measures I took to protect our marriage proved futile. One night during dinner, he talked about his workday. He shared another damaging confession, that he was having difficulty concentrating at work. Over the last month, he had been fantasizing about his twenty-something female coworkers during intimacy. I asked him if he had called his accountability partner from his sex addiction group, per our agreement. His response was, "I didn't think about it."

How could he "not think" about calling his accountability partner?! The truth was, he didn't want to think about it. The fact that I cared more about him getting well than he did made me angry at myself. I had been the one working hard doing my due diligence to protect him. Trying so hard to protect him left me little energy to focus on my own changes.

I made him spend the night in the upstairs bedroom. I needed time to think through what to do with his broken boundary. If I was to hold to our agreement, we would have to separate. This would make a third painful separation. I didn't hold out much hope that another separation would do any good. But I was frozen in fear and the pain of his confession weighed heavy on me.

That night I had a vivid dream. Laurel, Lynn, and I were at the airport. While heading to the gate to catch our flight, we stopped at a snack bar for gum. Realizing our flight was about to take off, we hurried towards the boarding area. Upon arriving at the gate, I noticed I had left my identification at the snack bar! In a panic, I ran back to get it and it wasn't there. It was lost! Lynn and Laurel came back to help me find it.

*I believe God was showing me I had lost my true identity. I had given up who I was for Jacob. Laurel and Lynn had done some hard work in counseling, and I was watching them both change as a result. Their strength and their ability to stand up to the wrongs made me want to do the same. Although it was more comfortable to support them and focus on their problems and healing, I realized that I was broken too. An interesting part of the dream was my friends had come back to help me. I was not alone in figuring out what steps I needed to take.*

*At the tea shop the next morning, I shared about Jacob's confession and my dream. Laurel and Lynn advised me to take time and ask God for direction. They helped me see my options. If I allowed Jacob to stay, what message would that give him? Our written agreement would mean nothing. I knew I would have to stick to my end of the agreement even though he hadn't.*

*With our first two separations, I had stayed and told Jacob to leave. He willingly and tearfully moved out but had regularly made excuses to come home. That made it difficult for me to focus on my own healing. This time I felt led to be the one to leave, to give myself more distance. But how would I afford to move out on my own?*

*When I got home, Jacob acted like a sad puppy who was in trouble with its owner. He regretted what he had done and apologized, professing his love for me and how sorry he was for hurting me again. He asked how he could make this better. I said I needed time to think and asked him to move out for thirty days. The stipulation was he couldn't contact me or come to the house. He agreed to do what I asked, and over and over again, said how sorry he was as he packed a bag. Before leaving he asked if he could at least call me and pray with me once a week. I relented and agreed. How do you turn down a husband who wants to pray with his wife?*

*The thirty days gave me time to pray for direction of where to go. At one of our weekly meetings, Lynn told me she had been thinking of renting out her basement. She offered to rent it to me for six months. I began packing what I would need to move out. Ashamed of Jacob's addiction, I could not tell our church friends and my family the real reason for our sep-*

aration. I said that he had problems with porn and had broken our agreement to get help. My heart was broken. I didn't want to leave but knew it was what I had to do.

Lynn encouraged me to sign up for Divorce Care. I reluctantly did so, even though I didn't feel I completely fit because I was separated, not divorced. A couple of really great friendships developed from that class and I learned more than I expected. I was still guarded in what I shared because I struggled to believe I would be accepted. My identity was still tied to being Jacob's wife and I felt ashamed for his choices.

During those six months, Jacob tried his best to pursue me. He asked me out on dates, bought me flowers and sent me cards. On our few dates, I was short with him. I felt irritated the whole time we were together. I started drinking wine in order to try and relax. I progressed from needing one glass to three to calm my anxiety and irritation of being with him. One night, he asked why I sounded mad at him when we talked. I hadn't seen it. I talked to Lynn about it afterwards. She said it was probably my gut instinct trying to tell me I didn't want to be around him. Listening to my gut was new to me. The less time I spent with him, the more clarity I gained about how I really felt.

Separating from Jacob gave me the time I needed to focus on myself. I had spent time working on Jacob's issues to no avail. Now, I began to pursue my personal healing in lieu of his.

Counseling helped identify why I was taking responsibility for Jacob instead of myself. I discovered I operated out of fear of abandonment, stemming from my alcoholic dad leaving us multiple times. I learned codependency from my mom's example of relating to him. These patterns showed up as I held onto love at any cost and stayed in manipulative and controlling relationships. I worked to re-integrate my mind and emotions and trust my gut. After years of ignoring and stuffing my emotions, I had to learn to tell myself the truth.

I was finally at a point of healing and invited my family over for Christmas. We had a wonderful time filled with laughter, gifts and games. Christmas afternoon, the girls said they were going for a drive. I had a hunch they were planning to go see "Papa Jacob." I slipped away to my room and called Jacob. He confirmed my hunch. They had asked if they could stop by, and he told them, "Yes." I was sooo angry I was shaking! He knew he was not allowed to see them!! Desperate, I begged him to leave before they got to the house. He said he'd think about it. I hung up and prayed he would leave.

The girls returned from their drive and we resumed our festivities. I wanted to ask them what they did but didn't want to ruin the day. I did my best to not think about whether Jacob had abided by my clear boundary. As soon as everyone left for home the next morning, I called and asked him if he left or stayed. He said he stayed but didn't invite them in. (As if that made it more palatable). They stood outside and talked for half-an-hour. I voiced my anger with him about his actions. He said maybe it would be better if we didn't talk for a while until I "cooled down." I said that was a good idea and angrily hung up the phone.

Shortly after that call, I set up a meeting with my pastor and his wife to seek guidance about divorce. But I became overwhelmed with confusion. I leaned on the help of my friends to prepare for the meeting. Lynn, Laurel and I met at the tea shop. Laurel suggested we role-play the conversation. I started talking, as if to the pastor, about Jacob's "issues with porn." Laurel stopped me, saying "What do you mean, porn?" At that moment, I honestly could not recall what Jacob had done.

As Lynn and Laurel listed the events, I heard them as if for the very first time. I felt sick to my stomach and in shock. They brought me back to reality by going over the timeline of discoveries about Jacob. Next, I repeated all of it back to them. Then, they had me write it down. The practice of writing out the truth kept me from dissociating from the painful memories. It was also a helpful tool I used to keep me on track as I told the pastor and his wife. My dream about losing my identity and my friends coming back to help me came true.

# 10

# So *THIS* is Love

The prince asked Cinderella to be his bride, and she said, "Yes!" for she **loved** him with all her heart, mind, and soul. It was a **dream come** true—a **new beginning**! Her friends decided to follow in her footsteps, and together they celebrated by sharing their stories. They wanted their **pain to have a purpose**, the saving of many lives.

## 10.1 Laurel

I didn't know it at the time, but the death of my parents marked the end of a very dark and painful season in my life. What followed was an unexpected season of blessings and new beginnings.

It started with a change of address. Mike and I moved out of the "smelly" house we'd lived in for seventeen years, into a home better suited to our stage of life. Situated near some wooded trails, it sits on a hill and has a beautiful view of the surrounding valley. At night, we often sit on the deck mesmerized by the glowing, twinkling city lights below.

At about the same time, I stepped down from my pastoral role at the church. Feeling called to help other victims of sexual abuse, I began writing my story and volunteering as a group leader for Sexual Abuse Victims Anonymous or SAVAnon. Allowing God to use my story to help others is very rewarding.

But my biggest blessing continues to be the relationships in my life. Mike and I weathered some very difficult storms during my recovery and our relationship was strengthened as a result. The same could be said of my relationship with Kelsey and Kenney. I am thankful that my childhood dream of having a family that loves God and loves each other has come true. Laughter, joy, love, and peace flood my home and life on a regular basis.

Life is good, but not always easy. Many of us who have a history of repressed childhood sexual abuse live with the belief we are one recollection away from our worst memory. That is certainly true for me. Occasionally, new memories of my past emerge, usually uninvited. When that happens, I apply the keys I shared in this book and grieve the loss. I mourn, but I don't lose hope, because my Savior lives. I can face each day because I know He is there to help me through it.

## 10.2 Jillian

Jillian's life has also gone through some dramatic changes. After her last separation from Jacob, she moved out of Lynn's basement into a beautiful daylight rancher. Her rent is less than a one-bedroom apartment! The owners,

relatives of an elderly client, wanted to bless Jillian. In fact, they have adopted her as extended family, and now include her in holiday celebrations and family vacations. There is nothing Jillian enjoys more than travel! In the last three years, she has been to China, Alaska, Greece, London, San Francisco, and Egypt! She even rode a camel! Who can say that?

*Jillian:*

*"My relationship with Jacob ended. It took being isolated from his manipulation to stay in reality. I found the courage to tell my daughter and her family the truth about Jacob. Instead of porn, I was able to state the problem as a sexual attraction to children. Their response surprised me. They didn't reject me but were empathetic. It turned out my fear of losing those relationships was unfounded. My disclosure and authenticity actually brought us closer together.*

*I also have a new job with a great company and have started leading a small group of women at my new church. Despite many unknowns, I am no longer living in fear of what the future might bring and am enjoying my life!"*

## 10.3 Lynn

Recently, I got some exciting news. Lynn was engaged! Not to brag, but I'm largely responsible. After I urged her to buy a boat, I got Lynn "hooked" on fishing. When Kevin, an avid fisherman, was asked by a mutual friend whether he'd like to meet a gal who also liked to fish, he readily agreed. After a successful blind date, they struck up a friendship and a romance blossomed. Two years have passed, and I'm happy to say she is on the verge of a new beginning. God is blessing her with a new husband and expanded family.

*Lynn:*

*"Dating Kevin was both exciting and terrifying. It made sense at first that dating made me anxious. After all, it had been thirty years and I was out of practice! But time and his apparent interest did not*

*improve my feelings. I started back in counseling when the symptoms of anxiety worsened, and learned I had PTSD. Dating triggered old fears of rejection and abandonment. In counseling, I was able to revisit the truth of what happened to me and how it affected my heart, this time in the context of learning to trust a man again. Instead of running, I had to stay in the relationship and let it play out with a different outcome.*

*Getting married is a dream come true. I have longed for a shared life and love that lasts and am looking forward to that with Kevin. But I am also seeing that longing fulfilled in other relationships. A year ago, I was in the delivery room as my first granddaughter was born. She has wound her way into my heart, and some of my favorite times are now spent watching her discover and master new things. Viewing life through her reactions opens my eyes to the joy present in small things. Tears come easily, but so does laughter, and when music plays, she drops everything and dances her heart out. She is reminding me to embrace life as a new adventure, move through my feelings, and take time to celebrate."*

## 10.4 Saying "Yes" to the Dress

Recently, Jillian and I had the privilege of going with Lynn to pick out her wedding dress. Although the two of us were optimistic and confident Lynn would find "the one," Lynn seemed skeptical. Walking through the doors of the large bridal boutique, she said, "You don't know how hard it is for me to find a dress that fits."

We ignored her insecurities. Completely. Once inside the doors, I bolted to the sale rack, and started pulling styles I thought Lynn would like. Jillian accompanied Lynn to a row of dresses recommended by her store-appointed stylist. In no time at all, we had a stack of dresses for her to try on.

Lynn disappeared inside her dressing room while Jillian and I took a seat nearby. As we waited for Lynn's first reveal, several brides-to-be emerged from adjacent rooms smiling and twirling as they looked at their reflections in the mirror and consulted with their friends and family. It was fun to watch.

But, after what seemed like an unusual amount of time, Lynn opened her dressing room door and stepped out in her street clothes. She appeared embarrassed and said, "My dressing room doesn't have a mirror inside, I can't see how I look."

Lynn has a great figure; I couldn't imagine any dress looking bad on her. But we sympathized, and the store attendant moved her to the back of the store, where there was a more private dressing room with a mirror on the inside and outside!

For the next three hours, Lynn tried on dress after dress. Many of them looked wonderful, even stunning on her. But you never would have known this by looking at her face. The longer the search, the sadder she got. I kept saying, "We're getting closer!" because we were. Each rejected dress gave us clues to what she liked and disliked. But I could tell Lynn didn't believe me.

Finally, Lynn's store appointed stylist asked her to reconsider a strapless dress, she felt strongly the one she had in mind might work. Reluctantly, Lynn agreed and emerged from her dressing room, this time lingering in front of the mirror. Our hearts leapt, could it be...? The stylist grabbed a champagne sash and adorned it around her waist. Lynn beamed, and we all cheered! Then, I grabbed a fur stole from a nearby rack and draped it around her shoulders. Lynn took one look in the mirror and started to cry happy tears of joy. She liked what she saw and said "yes" to the dress.

Later, as I pondered Lynn's search for a bridal gown, I realized her feelings mimicked those we felt as we intentionally took steps that led to our inner transformation.

- We began lacking self-esteem and the ability to see ourselves the way others did.
- We struggled with shame, fearing what others would think about us if our pasts were exposed.
- Many times, we got stuck, and needed the help of experts to progress.

- The journey was longer and harder than expected. It was the encouragement and support of our friends that kept us going.
- Our transformation was complete when the shame, insecurities, and fear we used to wear as a victim of abuse didn't fit us anymore. Secure in our new identity, we felt comfortable being authentic, strong and confident.

Though our lives are not in any way perfect, we all have much to be thankful for. We are moving forward with life. Our stories do have a **fairy-tale ending** even though it's not the one we originally hoped and prayed for.

The healing we've experienced isn't unique to us; it's available to everyone. You can take a similar journey; you don't have to stay a victim. God is inviting you to step out of that role; He has a rescue plan for your specific situation. All that is needed is a decision on your part. Are you willing to take the next step?

Maybe our relationship with God sounds foreign to you. I'm not sure if you realize this, but you are loved, wanted, and chosen too. If you've never done so, maybe your first step is to respond to God's love by talking to Him in prayer. Simply:

**Ask** for His forgiveness; all of us have fallen short.

**Believe** in Jesus, that He is your only hope of rescue.

**Confess** that Jesus is Lord; He's in charge and has your best interest at heart.

When we walk with Jesus, He promises to use even the bad things that happen to us for good. There is always hope for a fairy-tale ending.

## 10.3 Love Is A Catalyst for Change

Lynn, Jillian and I know this hope exists because we are familiar with Jesus' story. Before we ever experienced the trauma of abuse, Jesus did. But He did it willingly, because He loved us. It was part of God's rescue plan.

- Jesus chose to come as a willing **servant**.
- He was **abused** by those He loved and came to help.

- He knew His identity and value as God's **beloved** son, and loved people—even His enemies.
- He became **overwhelmed** with sorrow, sweating drops of blood in agony, knowing His midnight was approaching.
- **Ashamed.** He was falsely accused, beaten, publicly humiliated, spit on, stripped naked and nailed to a cross.
- A select few stood by and **supported** Him, but many abandoned Him during His hour of need.
- He became the innocent **scapegoat** when He died, willingly taking the blame we deserve.
- By overcoming death, He holds the **key** to unlock the doors that hold us captive.
- He returned to heaven to be with His Father and left us with His powerful Holy Spirit to **transform** us from the inside out.
- He will come again in **victory** for His bride, all who have accepted His invitation, and they will be with Him forever. There will be a celebration, like a wedding, and a new beginning will follow.

We are no longer victims; we are survivors of *Love Gone Wrong*. Jesus has rescued us and is the great love story of our lives. He says to us:

"Get up, my darling.
Let's go away, my beautiful one.
Look, the winter is past.
The rains are over and gone.
Blossoms appear through all the land.
The time has come to sing."[53]

# CONCLUSION:

Dear Reader,

If I only knew...

Some things seem a lot clearer in retrospect. From this vista, looking back on my long winding journey, I can see the roadblocks and diversions I might have avoided. There are some things I would do differently if I knew then what I know now. Maybe they will help you.

If I only knew, I would pay attention to red flags before I give my heart...

listen more to people I trust who disagree with my choice

look for actions to back up words that tell me what I want to hear

learn from history; past behavior is the best predictor of the future

If I only knew, I would share my shameful secrets...

telling someone else helps me stay in reality

authenticity connects me to people who can help

rehearsing the truth out loud, using the correct words, moves me to action

If I only knew, I would give myself more space...

separateness and safety clear up my confusion

proximity causes me to get sucked in by manipulation

working on the relationship keeps me from working on myself

If I only knew, I would maintain my friendships...

leaving friends behind disconnects me from my own history

people I want to run from may be triggering something deeper that needs attention staying in relationship was key in helping me change

I want you to know that you are not alone. It is not up to you, or even possible to figure out how to change all by yourself. Cinderella needed magical help from her fairy godmother to achieve a new identity. I found my supernatural help in the person of Jesus Christ, and you can too.

Jesus extends an invitation to you. "Here I am! I stand at the door and knock. If anyone hears my voice and opens the door, I will come in" (Revelation 3:20). Jesus is a gentleman; He does not force His way into our lives. Shame acts like a bolt on the door of our hearts; we hide behind closed doors and isolate ourselves from the One who can help us. It is up to us to turn the key and let Jesus in.

Forgiveness opens the door into our hearts. Then we can ask Jesus to transform us into the person we are meant to be. Doing so might sound something like this...

*Jesus, I ask for your forgiveness. I've been hurt but also responded in ways that I regret. I know You understand, because You were rejected and abused, but handled it perfectly. I give my life completely to You and ask for Your power to help me change.*

Once you've opened the door to Jesus, no one can ever shut it. You are free to come out from hiding and step into your happily-ever-after with Him—different than you imagined it, but even deeper and more meaningful than you ever dreamed.

Sincerely,

Lynn

# AFTERWORD

# Repressed Memories

Repressed memories are memories that have been unconsciously blocked due to being associated with a high level of stress or trauma. Trauma, by definition, is unbearable, intolerable and life changing. "Research from Neuroscience, The Study of the Brain," has revealed that trauma produces actual physiological changes, including a recalibration of the brain's alarm system, and an increase in stress hormone activity.

Most combat soldiers, rape victims and children who have been molested tend to shut down because the emotions are so overwhelming that the individual can only deal with them in small doses. They become so upset when they think about what they experienced, that they try to push it out of their minds, trying to act as if nothing happened and move on. For ongoing sexual abuse, this shut-down state may last for the entire time that the abuse occurred.

The term "repressed memory" is sometimes compared to the term "dissociative amnesia," which is defined in *The Diagnostic and Statistical Manual of Mental Disorders, Fifth Edition* (DSM-5) as an inability to recall autobiographical information. Some victims describe being outside their own experience, for example in the wall, watching someone being raped.

This is an example of dissociation; the client must dissociate from the sexual assault to survive it.

Sexual trauma in particular is viewed by a chamber of therapists as being especially susceptible to repression (Loftus, 1993). Psychologists and therapists who have witnessed clients remembering repressed experiences of childhood abuse argue that the memories are real, vivid, detailed and reliable.

Offenders tell victims many different things to silence them. For example: "This is our secret." "You are my favorite." Or the offender might say, "Don't tell your mom, or I will kill her." Or "Don't tell anyone, if you do, I will kill your dog." Or "No one will believe you." Or "You will get in trouble." The list goes on. Sex offenders are proficient in finding ways to silence their victims. It's another reason that victims learn to dissociate and compartmentalize their memories, thoughts and feelings.

Other victims try to tell but are met with resistance. "Don't worry about it." "Things like that could never happen in our family." "How could you ever think of such a terrible thing?" "Don't let me hear you say anything like that again." Roland Summit, M.D., from "The Child Sexual Abuse Accommodation Syndrome," describes the implications of sexual abuse so well. Initiation, intimidation, stigmatization, isolation, helplessness and self-blame depend on a terrifying reality of child sexual abuse. The average child never tells.

It takes tremendous energy to keep functioning while carrying the memory of terror and the shame of utter weakness and vulnerability. The part of the brain that is devoted to ensuring our survival (deep below our rational brain) is not very good at denial. Long after a traumatic experience is over, it may be reactivated at the slightest hint of danger and mobilize disturbed memories.

Some survivors of sexual abuse have memories of being abused as a child during their first adult sexual experience. One client told me she started having memories when she became pregnant. Others don't remember until later in life. They might have body memories, flashbacks or nightmares that precipitate memories of sexual abuse.

There isn't a cookie-cutter, one-size-fits-all way that survivors start remembering. It doesn't happen all at once. Healing from trauma such as sexual abuse happens in stages. Eventually, the survivor finds ways to put the past behind them, regulate their emotions, and build a stable life.

When the fear, anger, sadness, helplessness and heartache suddenly reemerge, the individual should sit with those emotions and allow them to come out. The individual now has the strength to cope with those emotions instead of stuffing them. That's why it is so important to get into therapy with a seasoned psychologist or therapist who specializes in sexual abuse/assault.

Several years ago, Elizabeth Loftus conducted research to work out repressed memories and whether some are false memories. I was able to attend a seminar where Elizabeth and John Briere had a debate about this topic. Later, I talked personally with both of them. Elizabeth alluded to several inexperienced therapists who told their clients that based on their symptoms, he or she thought they had been sexually abused.

In terms of treatment, it is not appropriate for a psychologist or therapist to tell a client that he/she knows or believes the client was sexually abused. If a client talks about some of their memories, and they are trying to make sense of it, it is okay to ask, "Tell me more about what you recall." If the client says, "I think I was sexually abused," the psychologist can say, "It's a possibility, why do you think that?"

Is it possible to have false memories? Yes. In general, most victims of sexual abuse do not lie. I've seen some cases where I questioned the disclosure because the client wasn't able to give me very many details. These were cases where it was a divorce situation and a parent may have influenced the young child.

Sexual abuse is devastating for any child, teen or adult. The research has been consistent for many years. One out of three girls will be sexually abused by the age of eighteen. One out of four-to-five boys will be sexually abused by the age of eighteen.

Mary A. Dietzen, PhD

# RESOURCES

## Resources for Victims of Sexual Abuse or Assault (Laurel's Story)

1. National Sexual Assault Hotline: Call 800-656-HOPE (4673) or online rainn.org (Rape, Abuse, and Incest National Network).
2. Sexual Assault Support for the Military: Call 877-995-5247 or safehelpline.org.
3. National Suicide Prevention Hotline Call 800-273-8255 or suicidepreventionlifeline.org.
4. Contact your insurance company to find out who their preferred providers are nearby where you live that specialize in assessment and treatment of victims of sexual abuse.
5. Call law enforcement to report it if someone discloses to you that they've been sexually abused by someone outside the family.
6. Call Child Protective Services if a child or teenager reports that a family member (who lives with them) has sexually abused him or her.
7. Visit Sexual Abuse Victims Anonymous online at savanon.org for assistance in finding recovery and healing. SAVAnon believes healing happens best in the context of community. Any victim of sexual abuse or assault can join an eight-week recovery group at no cost.

## Resources for Victims of Domestic Violence (Lynn's Story)

1. National Domestic Violence Hotline 800-799-7233.

2. Call law enforcement to report any incident of domestic violence.

3. Shelter for Domestic Violence Survivors visit domesticshelters.org or ywca.org to find the local shelters or programs in your area.

4. ARMS (Abuse Recovery Ministry Services) at abuserecovery.org. ARMS holds healing programs for women who are experiencing domestic abuse and intervention programs for men and women who have used controlling or abusive behaviors. ARMS offers a free fifteen-week class designed to assist women in healing from current or past abusive or controlling relationship.

## Resources for Partners of those with Compulsive Sexual Behaviors (Jillian's Story)

1. For individuals and/or their partners who struggle with compulsive sexual behaviors (sexually deviant behavior), check with the providers (psychologists and therapists) in your area who specialize in this area. This includes compulsive masturbation and sexual attraction to children.

2. Abortion Anonymous (AbAnon) is a community of women and men who recognize and desire recovery from the emotional pain caused by abortion. Members participate in a free, eight-week recovery program. Go to: Abanon.org.

## PTSD (Post-Traumatic Stress Disorder) Symptoms

A. A traumatic event is reexperienced in at least one of the following ways:

1. Distressing memories of the event, including sudden flashes of scenes of the abuse that intrude at unexpected and unwelcome times, as well as enduring haunting memories of the abuse.

2. Recurrent distressing dreams about the event. For sexual abuse survivors, this includes nightmares that are about sexual abuse or menacing perpetrators.

3. Suddenly acting or feeling as if the event were happening now. Includes a sense of reliving the event, seeing an image of the

event as if it were real, and flashback episodes, even those that occur upon awakening or when intoxicated.

4. Intense distress when exposed to events that symbolize or resemble some part of the trauma, including anniversaries of the trauma. For example, many sexual abuse survivors have very negative feelings whenever sex is initiated because it reminds them of sexual abuse. Survivors also often react to seemingly inconsequential objects or events because these things remind them of the abuse. One woman reported a strong aversion to the odor of coffee because she was abused by her brother in the morning while her mother was busy brewing the coffee.

B. Avoidance of things that remind one of the trauma indicated by:

1. Efforts to avoid thoughts or feelings of the trauma, including thinking about, remembering, or dealing with any of the feelings about the sexual abuse.

2. Efforts to avoid activities or situations that remind one of the trauma. Many survivors are told they suffer from a disorder because they have little desire or interest in sex. In fact, they are avoiding an activity, sex, that reminds them of their abuse. Survivors will also avoid baths if they were abused in the bathtub, dentists if they were orally abused, or pelvic exams if the exposure reminds them of their abuse.

3. Amnesia for an important part of the trauma. Notice that this symptom does not apply to survivors who have complete amnesia with no memory at all of their abuse.

4. Markedly diminished interest in significant activities like work, relationships or recreation.

5. Feelings of detachment or estrangement from others.

6. Restricted range of feelings, including feeling only rage, pain, or numbness, as the absence of love feelings, joy or closeness.

7. Sense of foreshortened future, as in not expecting to have a long life, marriage or a career.

C. Symptoms of increased arousal, as in being wound up or tense, evidenced by:

1. Difficulty falling asleep or staying asleep.
2. Irritability or outbursts of anger.
3. Difficulty concentrating.
4. Hypervigilance, or always being exceptionally watchful of potential danger.
5. Exaggerated startle response, as in jumping or reacting strongly when surprised or frightened.
6. Physical reactions to something that reminds one of the trauma like sweating or feeling nauseated when seeing a sexual scene in a movie.

## Recommended Reading

*Rewriting Your Emotional Script* by Becky Harling

*Beauty for Ashes: Receiving Emotional Healing* by Joyce Meyer

*Total Forgiveness* by R.T. Kendall

*How to Forgive Ourselves Totally* by R.T. Kendall

*Codependent No More: How to Stop Controlling Others and Start Caring for Yourself* by Melody Beattie

*Safe People: How to Find Relationships That Are Good for You and Avoid Those That Aren't* by Dr. Henry Cloud and Dr. John Townsend

*Repressed Memories* by Renee Frederickson

*No More Christian Nice Girl* by Jennifer Deglar and Paul Coughlin

*Fooling Proofing Your Life* by Jan Silvious

*The Emotionally Destructive Relationship* by Leslie Vernick

*The Healing Timeline* by M.A. Thorp

*Boundaries in Marriage* by Henry Cloud and John Townsend

*Necessary Endings* by Henry Cloud

*Telling Yourself the Truth* by William Backus and Marie Chapman

# ACKNOWLEDGMENTS

With special thanks:

- To my daughter Kelsey, whose expertise and contributions made this book possible.
- To Rob Fischer, writer and editor. Your wisdom, guidance, and enthusiasm for writing blessed me tremendously.
- To Morgan James Publishing for your encouragement, coaching, and contributions to this book. Your partnership enabled me to get this message into the hands of those who need it.
- To my brother. Thank you for your  commitment to our relationship. I love you.
- To my Pastor and his wife. Your influence in my life, ministry, and health cannot be understated. Thank you for your perseverance and friendship.
- To my many friends and family members who gave input all along the way and believed in this project and its message.

# BIBLIOGRAPHY OF CLINICAL REFERENCES

Briere, John PhD and Catherine Scott, MD. *Trauma Therapy*. Thousand Oaks, CA: Sage Publications, Inc., 2006.

Finkelhor, David. *Child Sexual Abuse: New Theory and Research*. New York, NY: The Free Press, 1984.

Groth, A. Nicholas and H. Jean Birnbaum. *Men Who Rape: The Psychology of the Offender*. Cambridge, MA: Perseus Books, 1980.

Herman, Judith. *Trauma & Recovery*. New York, NY: Basic Books, 1997.

Malamuth, Neil M. and Edward Donnerstein, Editors. *Pornography and Sexual Aggression*. Orlando, FL: Academic Press, Inc., 1984.

Maltz, Wendy. *The Sexual Healing Journey*. New York, NY: HarperCollins, 2012.

Mason, Paul MS and Randi Kreger. *Stop Walking on Egg Shells: Taking Your Life Back When Someone You Care About Has Borderline Personality Disorder (Second Edition)*. Oakland, CA: New Harbinger Publications, Inc., 2010.

Ochberg, Frank M.D. Editor, *Post Traumatic Therapy and Victims of Violence*. New York, NY: Brunner/Mazel, Publishers, 1987.

Rothschild, Bobette. *The Body Remembers: The Psychology of Trauma and Trauma Treatment*. New York & London: W.W. Norton & Company, 2000.

Van Der Kolk, Bessel M.D. *The Body Keeps the Score*. New York, NY: Viking Penguin Books, 2015.

# ABOUT THE AUTHOR

Laurel Bahr was a registered nurse for over 17 years, pastor for 17 years, and survivor of sexual abuse. She is uniquely qualified to speak hope to anyone struggling with brokenness. She knows first-hand what it's like to feel paralyzed, unable to make progress and change.

By reading her story, victims of sexual abuse and domestic violence, and their loved ones, can benefit from the lessons learned through her recovery process. Readers will come away with increased awareness, compassion, hope and the courage to take a step towards their own healing. Laurel is currently a director of SAVAnon, Sexual Abuse Victims Anonymous, and resides in Spokane, Washington.

# ENDNOTES

1   Lia Mack, "What are Body Memories? And How to Heal them…#PTSD# Sexual Assault," Survivor Manual, August 17, 2015. http://www.survivor-manual.com/how-to-deal-with-body-memories-as-a-survivor-of-sexual-assault/.

2   Renee Fredrickson, PhD, *Repressed Memories—A Journey to Recovery from Sexual Abuse* (New York, NY: Simon & Schuster, 1992), p. 22.

3   Renee Fredrickson, PhD, p. 81.

4   D'Arcy Lyness, PhD, "Child Abuse," KidsHealth from Nemours, May 23, 2019. https://m.kidshealth.org/CHW/en/parents/child-abuse.html.

5   Committee for Children, "Early, Open, Often," May 23, 2019. https://www.earlyopenoften.org/get-the-facts/signs-of-sexual-abuse/.

6   Darkness to Light, "Child Sexual Abuse Statistics", May 23, 2019. https://www.d2l.org/wp-content/uploads/2017/01/Statistics_2_Perpetrators.pdf.

7   Center for Hope & Safety, "Warning Signs of an Abuser," May 23, 2019. https://hopeandsafety.org/learn-more/warning-signs-of-an-abuser/.

8   Sharie Stines, MBA, Psy.D, CATC-V, "Victims of Emotional Abuse," Psych Central, November 11, 2018, https://pro.psychcentral.com/recovery-expert/2016/07/victims-of-emotional-abuse/.

9   Renee Fredrickson, PhD, p. 20.

10  Renee Fredrickson, PhD, p. 77.

11  Paula Sandford, *Garlands for Ashes…Healing Victims of Sexual Abuse* (Tulsa, Oklahoma: Victory House Publishers, 1988), p.124.

12  Lynne Namka, Ed. D., "Scapegoating-An Insidious Family Pattern of Blame and Shame on a Family Member," Talk, Trust, and Feel Therapeutics, May

23, 2019. https://lynnenamka.com/narcissism/scapegoating-insidious-fami-ly-pattern/.

13  Ron Dias, *Cinderella* (New York, NY: Random House Children's Books, 2006), p. 9.

14  Genesis 50:20, New Living Translation, copyright © 1996, 2004, 2015 by Tyndale House Foundation.

15  "Trauma-Informed Care in Behavioral Health Services," NCBI, May 23, 2019. https://www.ncbi.nlm.nih.gov/books/NBK207191/.

16  Frank Meadows, LCSW, "Theophostic Healing Prayer," The Christian Broadcasting Network, May 23, 2019. http://www1.cbn.com/prayer/the-ophostic-healing-prayer.

17  Renee Fredrickson, PhD, p. 77.

18  Renee Fredrickson, PhD, p. 37-38.

19  Lydia Wood, "The Cycle of Abuse," Freedom K9 Project, October 11, 2016. https://www.freedomk9project.com/single-post/2016/10/11/The-Cy-cle-of-Abuse?gclid=CjwKCAiAqbvTBRAPEiwANEkyCPgjf8CjoasmE3Gy-3qyX2AF6IYMgAmn4rh0yEKskilJtlsTa0NieoRoCD0gQAvD_BwE.

20  Renee Fredrickson, PhD, p. 35.

21  Mayo Clinic, "Post-Traumatic Stress Disorder, July 6, 2018. https://www.mayoclinic.org/diseases-conditions/post-traumatic-stress-disorder/symp-toms-causes/syc-20355967.

22  Substance Abuse and Mental Health Services, "Triggers," May 23, 2019. https://www.mentalhelp.net/articles/triggers/.

23  Lydia Wood, "The Cycle of Abuse."

24  Paula Sandford, p. 122.

25  Leslie Vernick. *The Emotionally Destructive Relationship* (Eugene, Oregon: Harvest House Publishers, 2007), p. 163.

26  Paula Sandford, p.122.

27  Renee Fredrickson, PhD, p. 203.

28  Renee Fredrickson, PhD, p. 79.

29  Renee Fredrickson, PhD, p. 207.

30  Renee Fredrickson, PhD, p. 208.

31  John 11:35 NLT, *Holy Bible, New Living Translation*, copyright © 1996, 2004, 2015 by Tyndale House Foundation. Used by permission of Tyndale

House Publishers, Inc., Carol Stream, Illinois 60188. All rights reserved.

32 Dictionary.com, LLC, https://www.dictionary.com/browse/scapegoat

33 Lisa Thomson, "Scapegoating in Families-What We Need to Know," Lisa Thompson Live Blog, September 16, 2014, http://www.lisathomsonlive. com/scapegoating-in-families-what-we-need-to-know/

34 Renee Fredrickson, PhD, p. 203.

35 Renee Fredrickson, PhD, p. 207.

36 Leslie Vernick, p.161-162.

37 Paul Coughlin & Jennifer Deglar, *No More Christian Nice Girl* (Minneapolis, Minnesota: Bethany House, 2010), p.27)

38 Jan Silvious, *Foolproofing Your Life*, (Colorado Springs, Colorado: Water-Brook Press, 1998), p.189

39 Jan Silvious, p.194.

40 Zawn Villines, "Battered Woman Syndrome and Intimate Partner Violence," Medical News Today, 3 December 2018. https://www.medicalnewstoday.com/articles/320747.php.

41 Aris R., "Escalation," The National Domestic Violence Hotline, September 28, 2018. www.thehotline.org/2018/09/28/escalation/.

42 Renee Fredrickson, PhD, p. 59.

43 60 Minutes Advanced PTSD Therapy, YouTube, May 23, 2019. https:// www.youtube.com/watch?v=7frOWBiU8D4.

44 Renee Fredrickson, PhD, p. 125.

45 Renee Fredrickson, PhD, p. 77.

46 Renee Fredrickson, PhD, p. 60.

47 Numbers 6:24 KJV.

48 Numbers 6:24 NLT.

49 "Struggle is Good! I want to fly!" Accessed May 23, 2019. http://instructor. mstc.edu/instructor/swallerm/Struggle%20-%20Butterfly.htm.

50 "Pedophilia," Psychology Today, February 22, 2019. Psychologytoday.com/ us/conditions/pedophilia.

51 Jennifer Focht, "The Cycle of Domestic Violence," National Center for Health Research, accessed May 23, 2019. http://www.center4research.org/ cycle-domestic-violence/.

52 *The English Dictionary*, online version. https://www.google.com/

search?q=the+english+dictionary&oq=the+english+dictionary&aqs=-chrome..69i57j0l5.3623j0j7&sourceid=chrome&ie=UTF-8#dobs=subter-fuge.

53 Song of Songs 2:10-12, The Holy Bible, International Children's Bible® Copyright© 1986, 1988, 1999, 2015 by Tommy Nelson™, a division of Thomas Nelson.